teacher's friend
publications

MAPS!

The World
and
United States

P9-DGI-607

Current outline maps for all regions, countries and states

Copyright © 1991, 1996, 1999
Teacher's Friend Publications, Inc.
All rights reserved.
Printed in the United States of America
Published by Teacher's Friend Publications, Inc.
3240 Trade Center Dr., Riverside, CA 92507

ISBN-0-943263-20-4

Table of Contents

HOW TO USE THIS "MAPS!" BOOK! 5

COUNTRIES OF THE WORLD 7
THE CONTINENTS 8
THE BRITISH ISLES 9
NORTHERN EUROPE 11
SOUTHERN EUROPE 13
THE MIDDLE EAST 15
AFRICA 17
ASIA 19
SOUTHEAST ASIA, JAPAN AND MALAYSIA 21
AUSTRALIA AND PACIFIC ISLANDS 23
RUSSIA AND COMMONWEALTH OF INDEPENDENT STATES 25
ANTARCTICA 27
SOUTH AMERICA 29
MEXICO AND CENTRAL AMERICA 31
THE UNITED STATES 33
CANADA 35
THE ARCTIC AND GREENLAND 37
THE WESTERN AND EASTERN HEMISPHERES 39

MY COUNTRY REPORT! 40

THE UNITED STATES 41
        ALABAMA 43
        ALASKA 44
        ARIZONA 45
        ARKANSAS 46
        CALIFORNIA 47
        COLORADO 48
        CONNECTICUT 49
        DELAWARE 50
        FLORIDA 51
        GEORGIA 52
        HAWAII 53
        IDAHO 54
        ILLINOIS 55
        INDIANA 56
        IOWA 57
        KANSAS 58
        KENTUCKY 59
        LOUISIANA 60
        MAINE 61
        MARYLAND AND WASHINGTON, D.C. 62
        MASSACHUSETTS 63
        MICHIGAN 64

MINNESOTA 65
MISSISSIPPI 66
MISSOURI 67
MONTANA 68
NEBRASKA 69
NEVADA 70
NEW HAMPSHIRE 71
NEW JERSEY 72
NEW MEXICO 73
NEW YORK 74
NORTH CAROLINA 75
NORTH DAKOTA 76
OHIO 77
OKLAHOMA 78
OREGON 79
PENNSYLVANIA 80
RHODE ISLAND 81
SOUTH CAROLINA 82
SOUTH DAKOTA 83
TENNESSEE 84
TEXAS 85
UTAH 86
VERMONT 87
VIRGINIA 88
WASHINGTON 89
WEST VIRGINIA 90
WISCONSIN 91
WYOMING 92

THE THIRTEEN COLONIES 93
REGIONS OF THE U.S. 95
MAJOR U.S. RIVERS AND LAKES 96
MAJOR U.S. MOUNTAIN RANGES AND DESERTS 97
U.S. TIME ZONES 98

MY STATE REPORT! 99

STATE INFORMATION 102

How To Use This "Maps!" Book!

The outline maps contained in this book were designed to reinforce and expand the geographical knowledge of your students. The bold, simple outlines leave a great deal of freedom for you and your students to use the maps in a variety of ways. These maps can be used at all grade levels.

Here are a few suggestions for using maps in the classroom:

- Use the maps to note major cities, rivers and lakes, mountain ranges and deserts, agriculture, national parks, points of interest, etc.

- Each country's or state's physical or political information can be noted using a student-made legend. (Each map contains a blank area for students to note their own legend symbols or colors.)

- Have each student use one of the maps for the cover page of his or her report.

- Enlarge one of the maps to teach current events or note specific information about your own state.

- Create student-made atlases. Have each student staple the maps into a booklet for future individual reference.

Ideas for Students Using the World Maps:

- Use one of the maps as the basis for a research report. Assign each student a different country or area of the world. Ask them to find out the customs, language, government, major cities, resources, etc. (Many of these elements can be noted on the maps.) The reports can be displayed with the appropriate maps on the class bulletin board.

- When teaching current events, give each student their own copy of the specific area of the world and ask them to note the areas being discussed.

- Color each country a different color.
- Locate and write in the capital cities of each country.
- Draw in the major rivers, lakes, deserts and mountain ranges.
- Using symbols, note the agriculture and natural resources of each area.
- Note the largest population areas.
- Show the average rainfall and temperature of each area.
- Note the different kinds of animals, birds and fish naturally found in each area or country.
- Show important points of interest, such as volcanoes, waterfalls, canyons or historical monuments (the Great Wall of China, Pyramids of Egypt, etc.)

Ideas for Students Using the Map of the United States:

- Write in each state's name.
- Indicate the original thirteen colonies.
- Color in the Union and Confederate states pertaining to the Civil War.
- Write in each state's capital city.
- Mark the route west used by Lewis and Clark or the Pony Express.
- Indicate the year each state was accepted into the Union.
- Draw in major rivers, deserts, lakes and mountain ranges.
- Show the various time zones.

Ideas for Students Using the Individual State Maps:

- Assign each student to research one individual state. Have them use the map of that state as the basis for their report. (You might want students to use the "My State Report!" forms located at the back of this book.)   The reports can be displayed with the state maps on the class bulletin board.

- The individual state maps (with the state names removed) can be used as flash cards with students identifying each state by it's shape. Extra points can be awarded to those that can name the capital city and locate it on the classroom map.

- Write in each state's capital city and other major cities. (The "star" on each map indicates the location of that state's capital city.)
- Draw in major rivers, deserts, lakes and mountain ranges.
- Use symbols to show agriculture, natural resources, transportation and industry.
- Note the highest and lowest elevations.
- List each state's population, area (square miles), state flower, state bird and nickname.
- Indicate such national monuments as Mount Rushmore, The Grand Canyon and Yellowstone National Park.

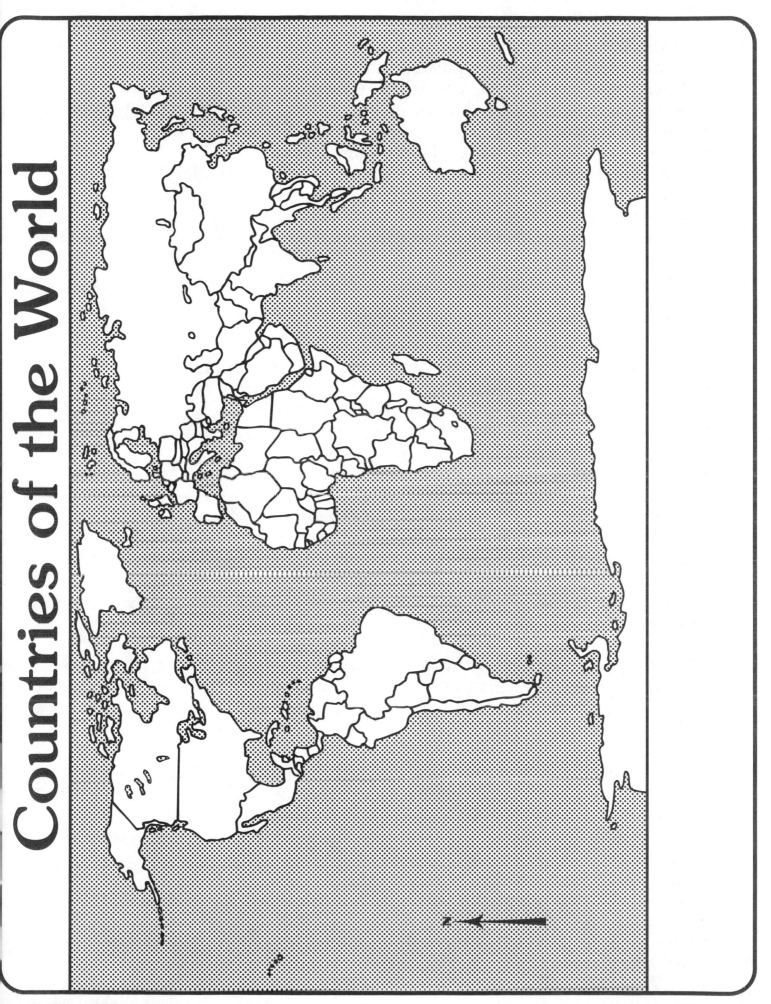

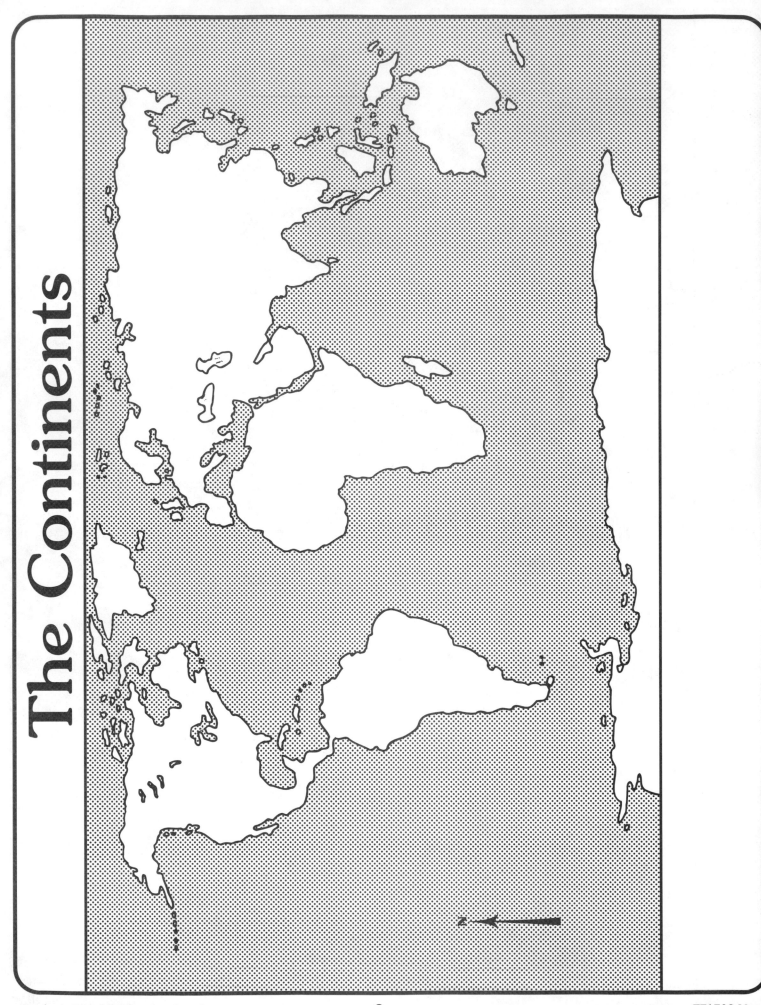

The Continents

The British Isles

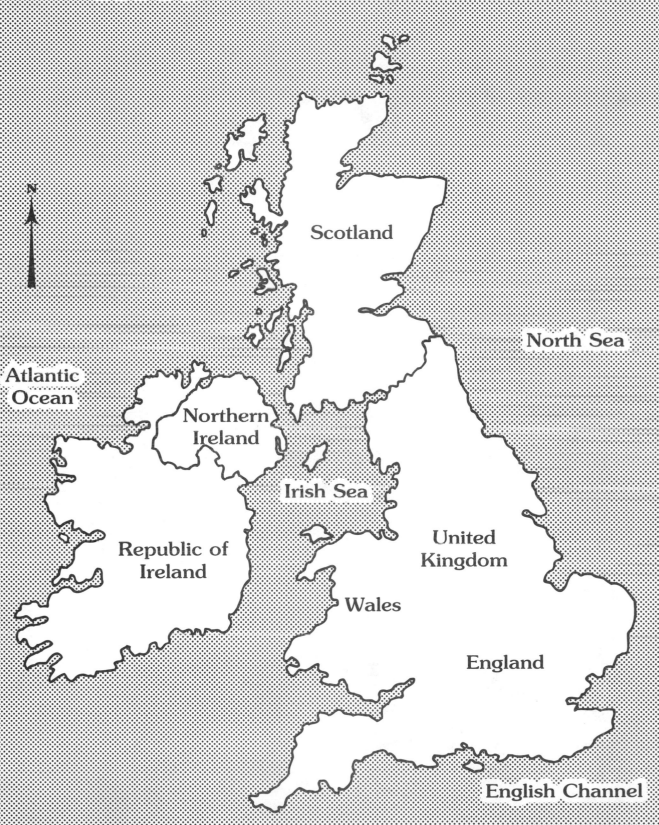

Shetland Islands

N

Scotland

North Sea

Atlantic Ocean

Northern Ireland

Irish Sea

United Kingdom

Republic of Ireland

Wales

England

English Channel

The British Isles

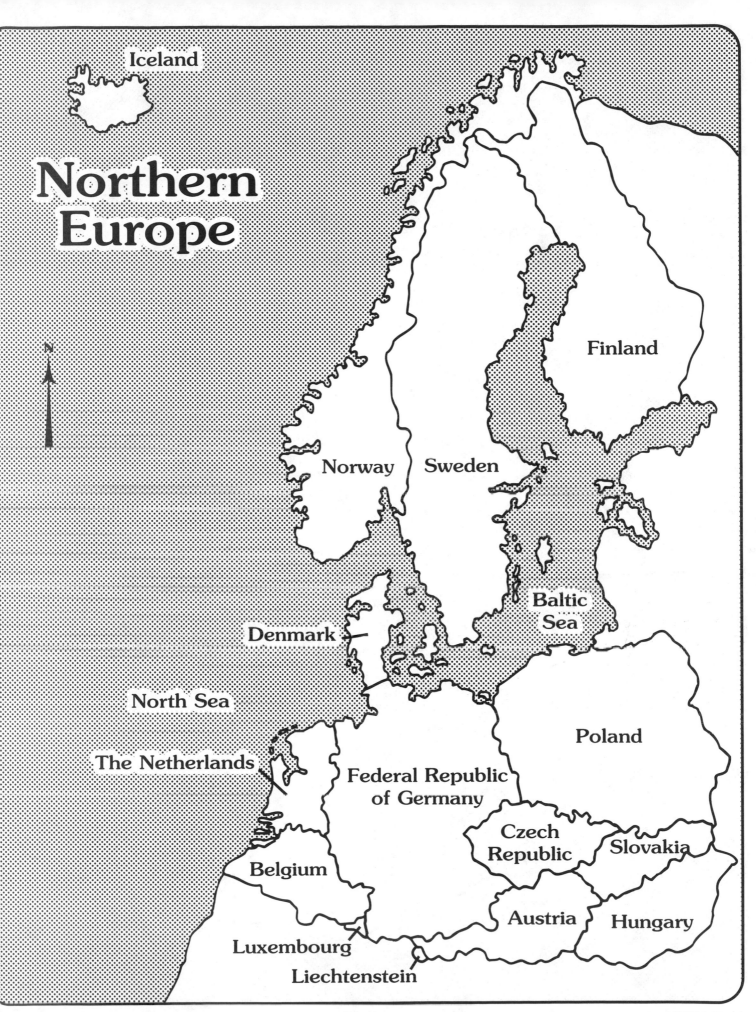

Northern Europe

Iceland

N

Norway   Sweden   Finland

Denmark   Baltic Sea

North Sea

The Netherlands   Poland

Federal Republic of Germany

Belgium   Czech Republic   Slovakia

Luxembourg   Austria   Hungary

Liechtenstein

Northern Europe

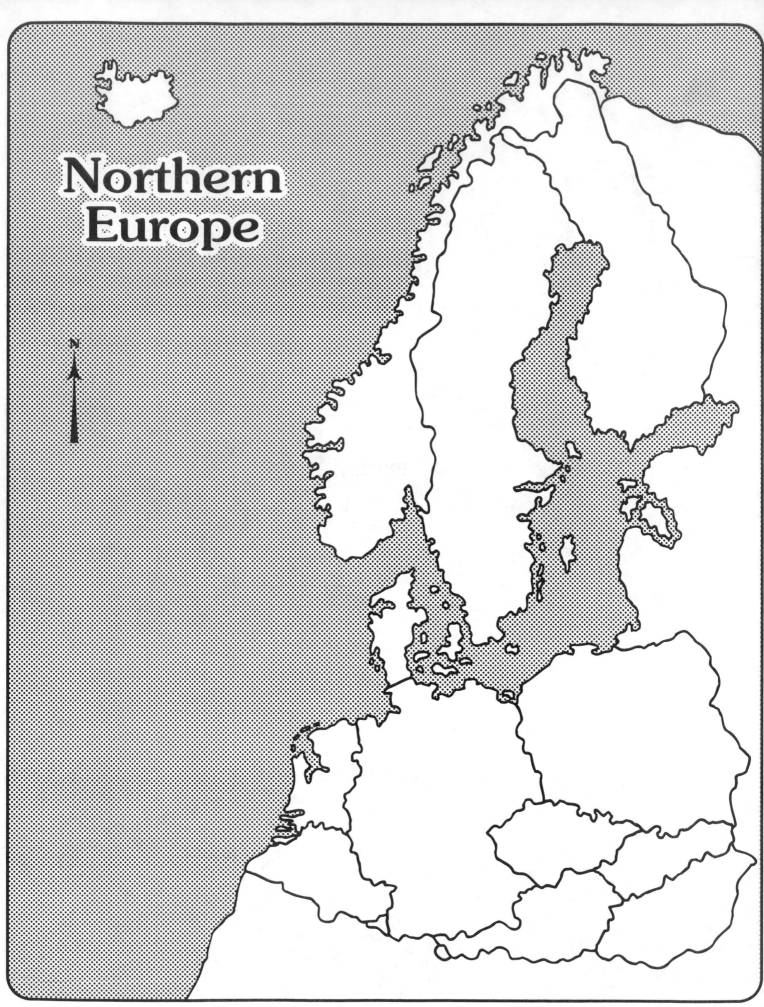

Southern Europe

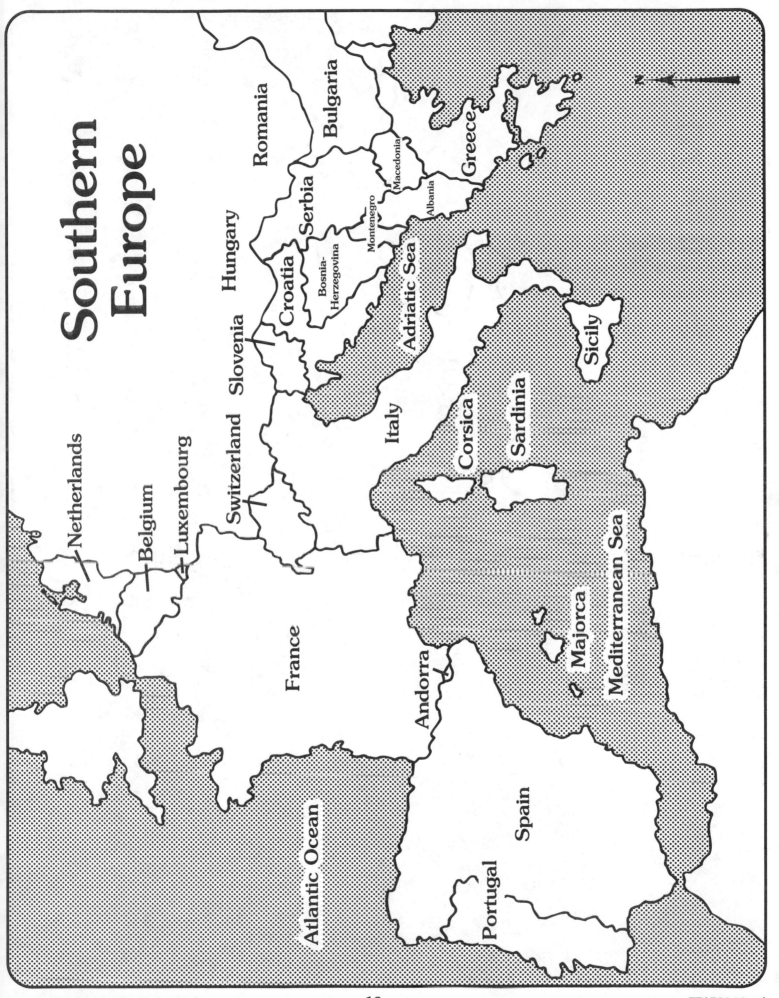

Netherlands

Belgium

Luxembourg

Switzerland

Slovenia

Hungary

Romania

Bulgaria

Croatia

Serbia

Bosnia-Herzegovina

Montenegro

Macedonia

Albania

Greece

Adriatic Sea

Italy

Corsica

Sardinia

Sicily

France

Andorra

Majorca

Mediterranean Sea

Atlantic Ocean

Portugal

Spain

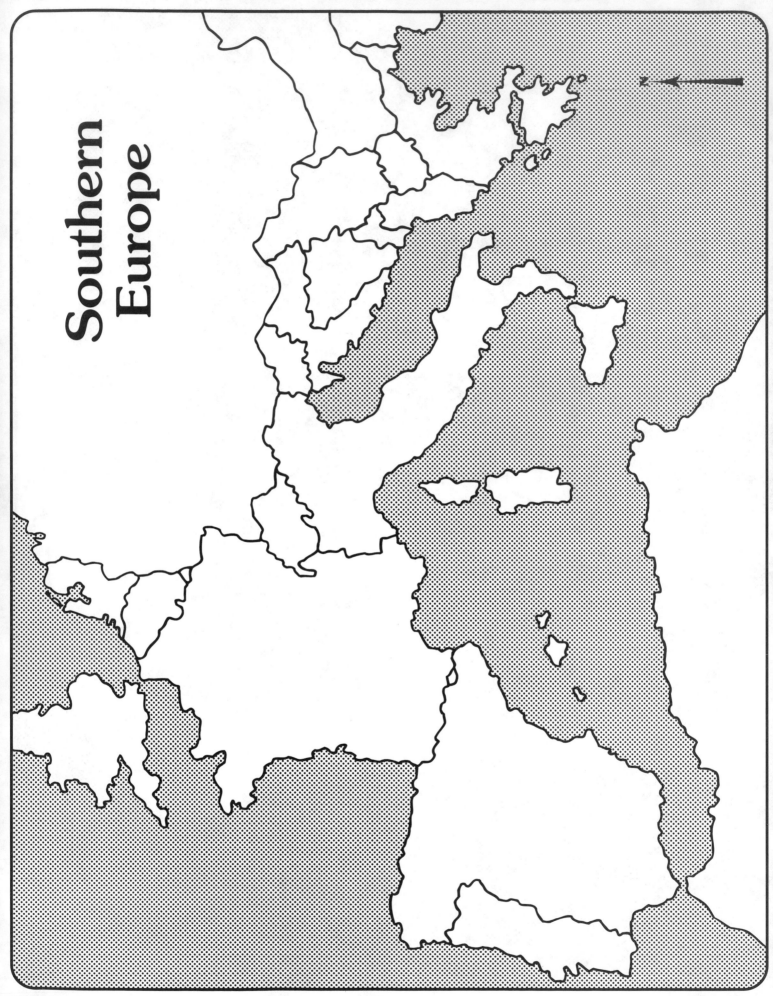

Southern Europe

The Middle East

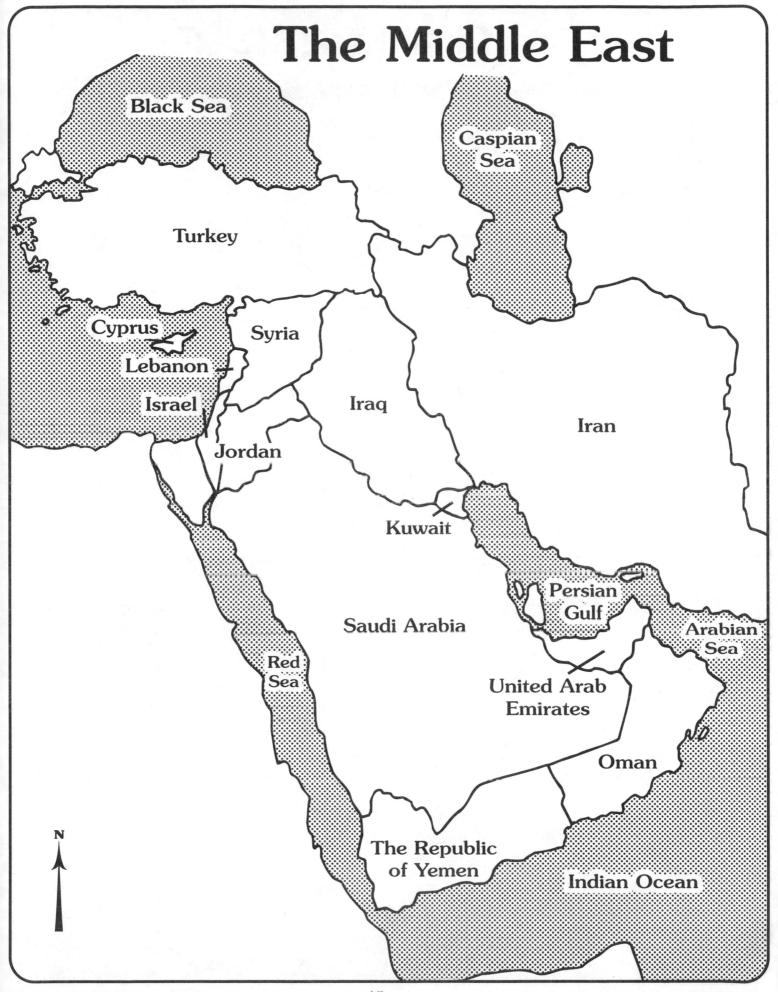

Black Sea

Caspian Sea

Turkey

Cyprus

Syria

Lebanon

Israel

Jordan

Iraq

Iran

Kuwait

Saudi Arabia

Persian Gulf

Arabian Sea

Red Sea

United Arab Emirates

Oman

The Republic of Yemen

Indian Ocean

N

The Middle East

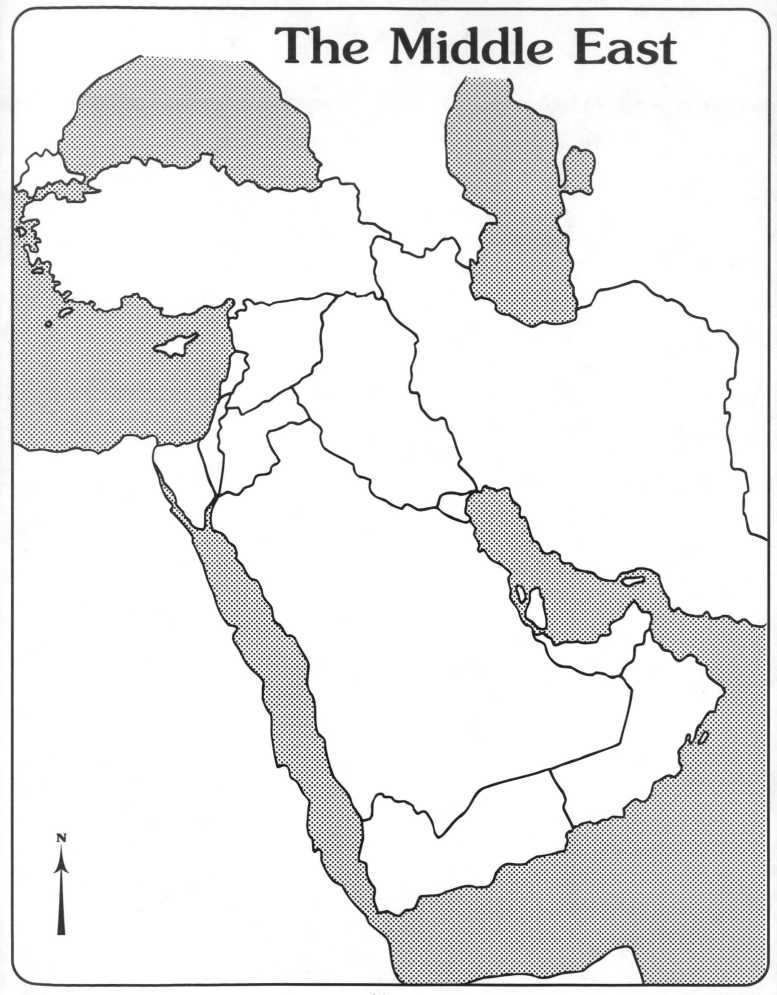

N

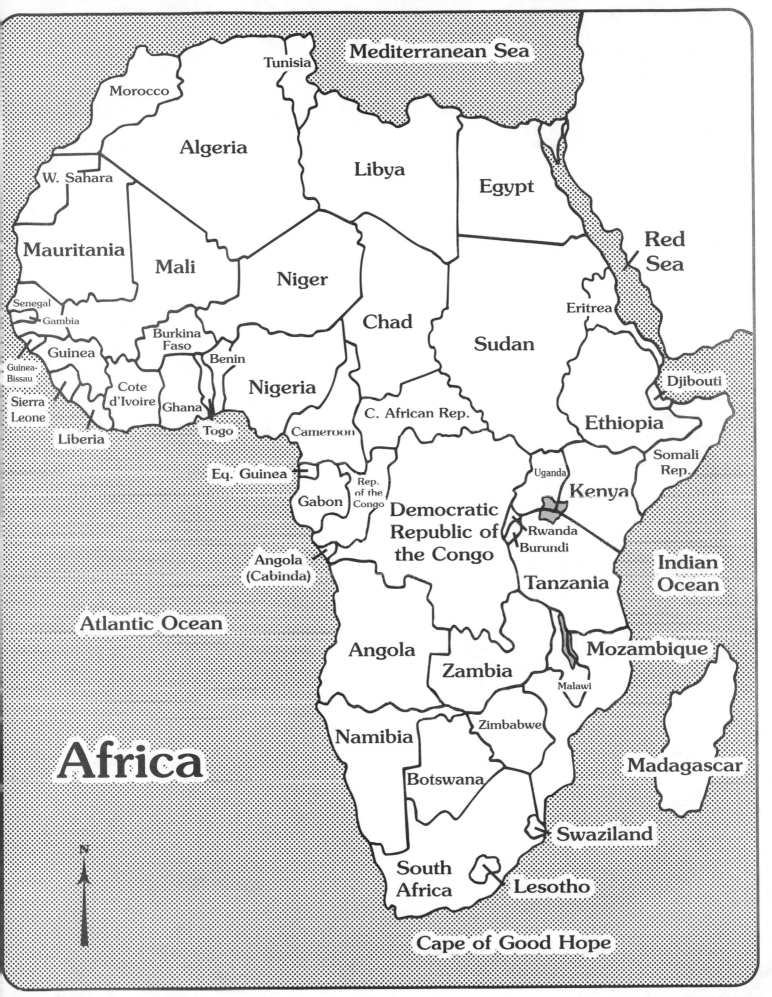

Mediterranean Sea

Morocco

Tunisia

Algeria

W. Sahara

Libya

Egypt

Red Sea

Mauritania

Mali

Niger

Chad

Eritrea

Sudan

Senegal

Gambia

Burkina Faso

Benin

Djibouti

Guinea

Guinea-Bissau

Cote d'Ivoire

Ghana

Togo

Nigeria

C. African Rep.

Cameroon

Ethiopia

Somali Rep.

Sierra Leone

Liberia

Eq. Guinea

Gabon

Rep. of the Congo

Uganda

Kenya

Democratic Republic of the Congo

Rwanda

Burundi

Angola (Cabinda)

Tanzania

Indian Ocean

Atlantic Ocean

Angola

Zambia

Malawi

Mozambique

Namibia

Zimbabwe

Madagascar

Africa

Botswana

Swaziland

N

South Africa

Lesotho

Cape of Good Hope

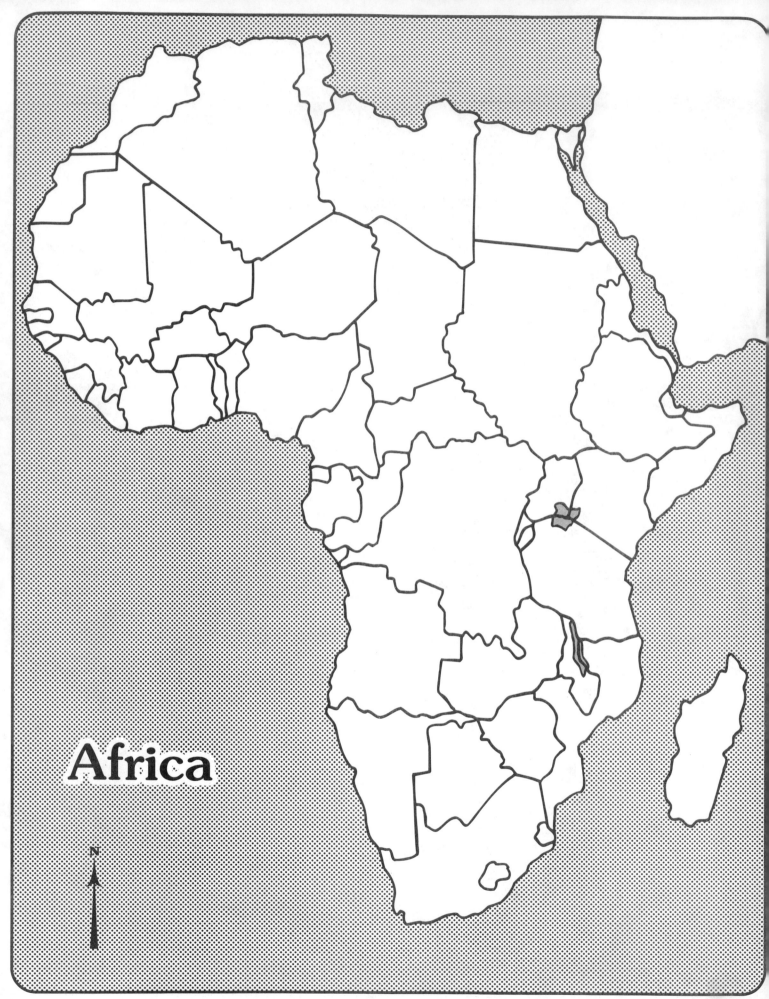

Africa

N

Asia

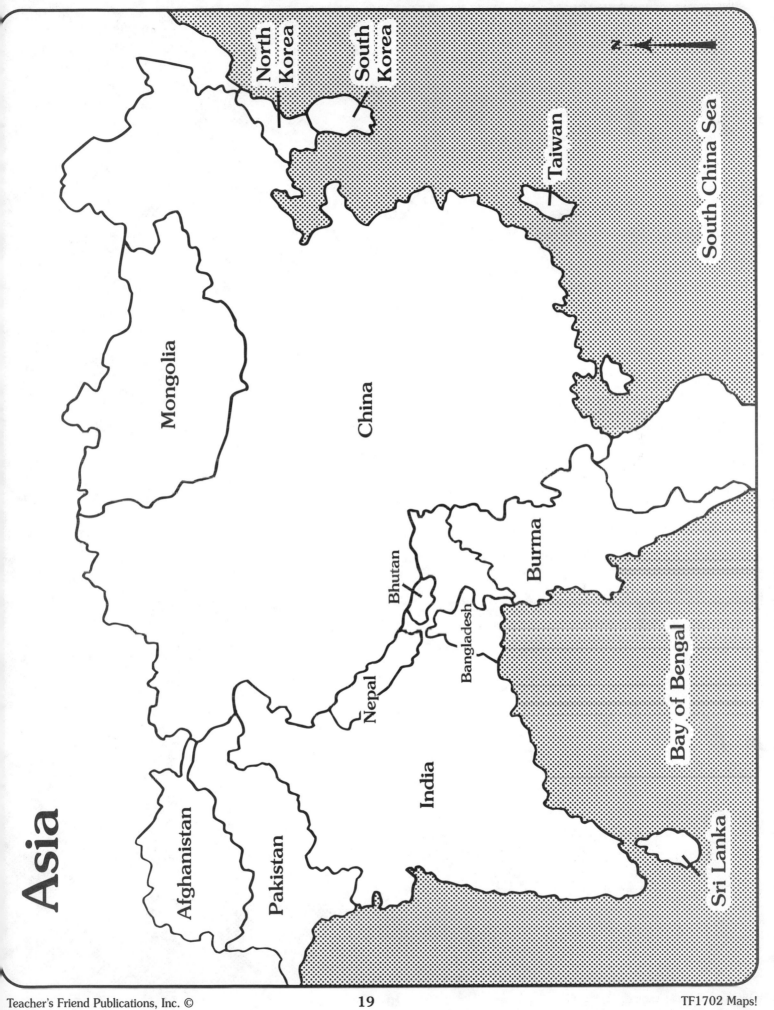

North Korea

South Korea

Taiwan

South China Sea

Mongolia

China

Bhutan

Burma

Nepal

Bangladesh

Bay of Bengal

Afghanistan

Pakistan

India

Sri Lanka

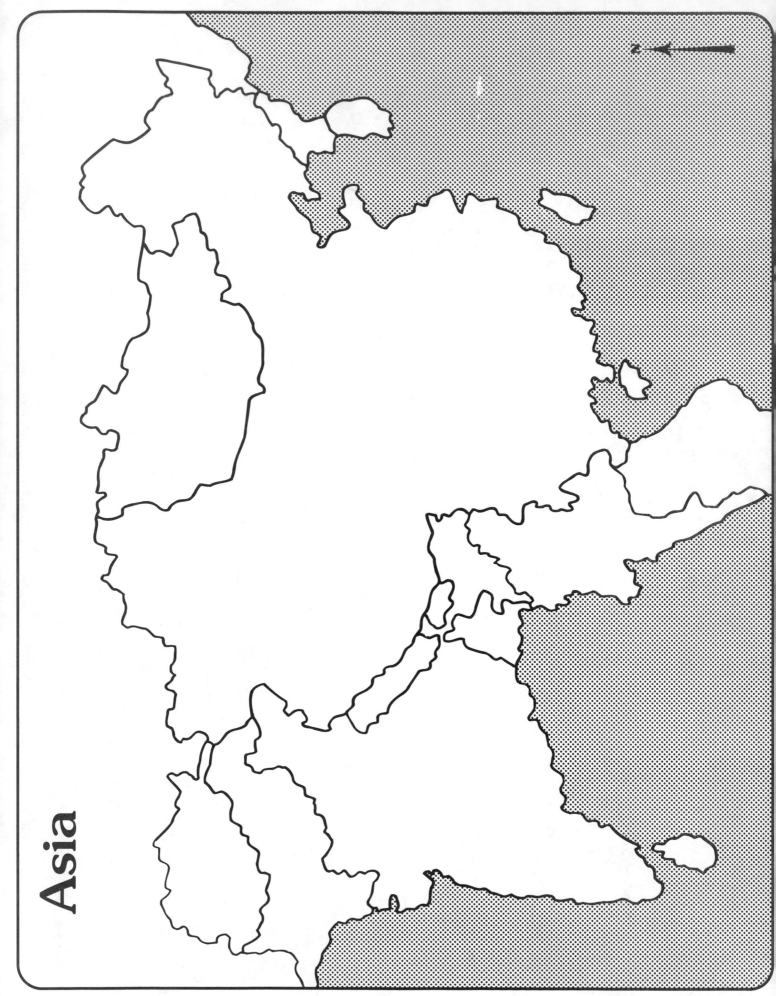

Asia

Southeast Asia, Japan and Malaysia

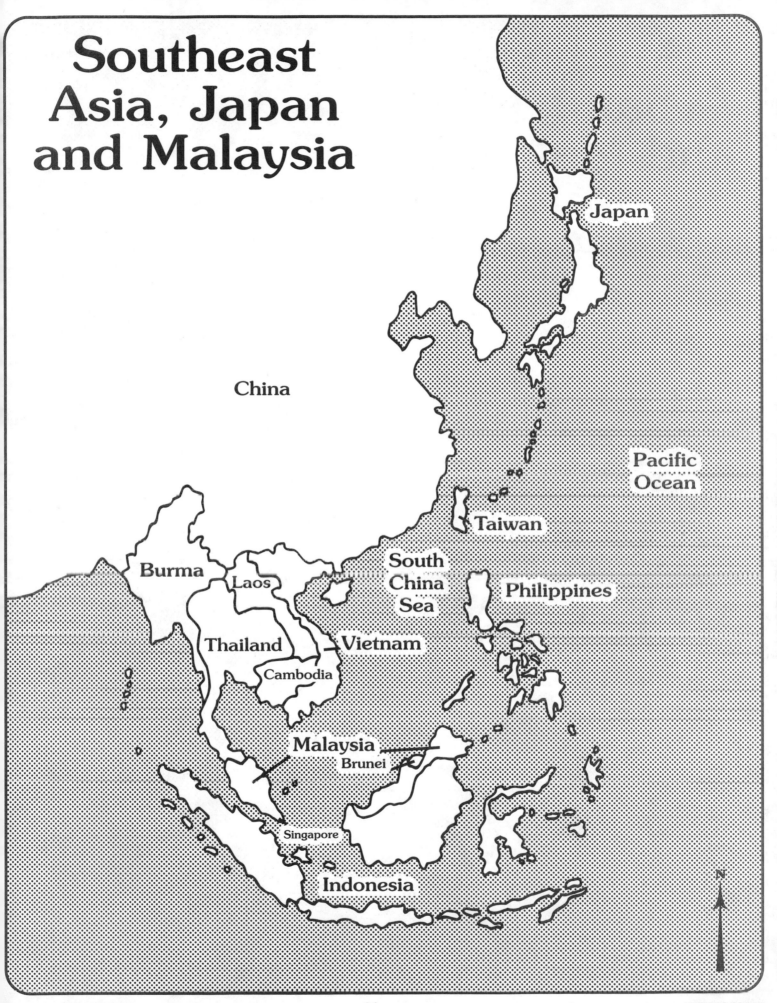

China

Japan

Pacific Ocean

Burma

Laos

Taiwan

South China Sea

Philippines

Thailand

Vietnam

Cambodia

Malaysia

Brunei

Singapore

Indonesia

N

Southeast Asia, Japan and Malaysia

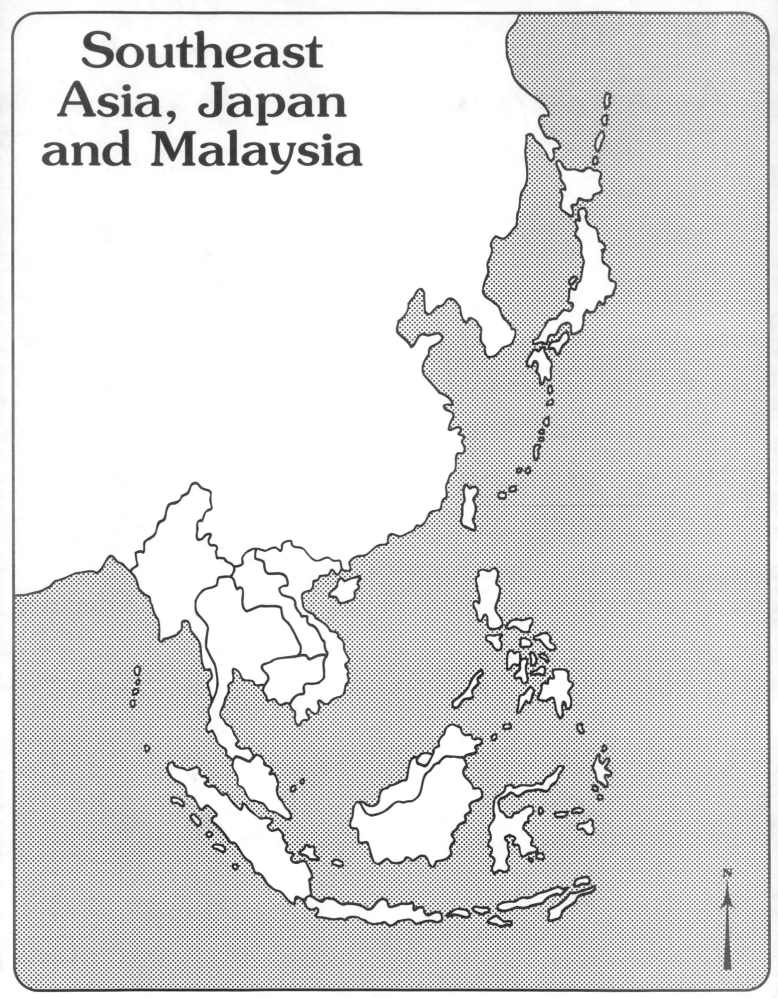

N

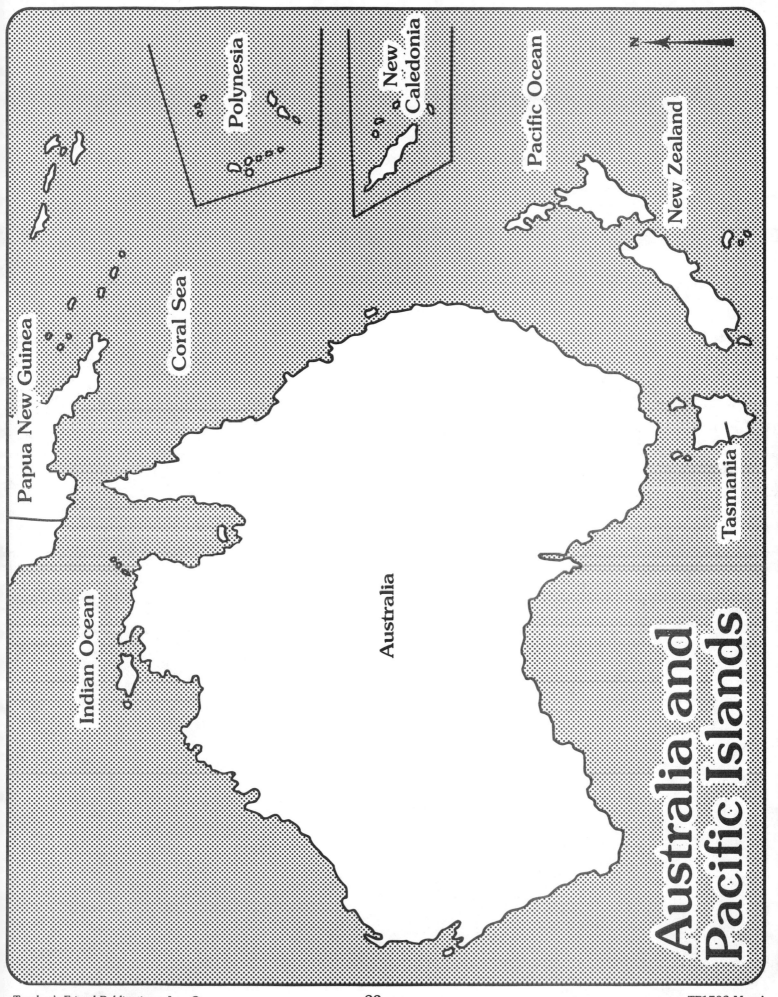

Polynesia

New Caledonia

Pacific Ocean

New Zealand

Papua New Guinea

Coral Sea

Tasmania

Indian Ocean

Australia

Australia and Pacific Islands

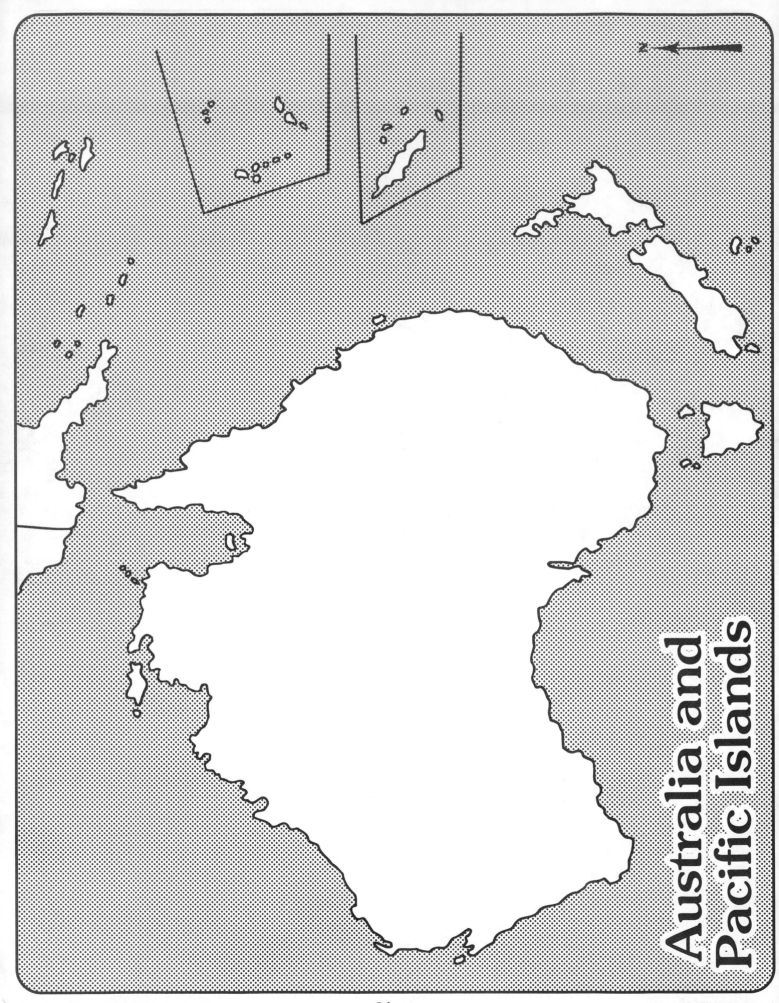

Australia and
Pacific Islands

Russia and Commonwealth of Independent States

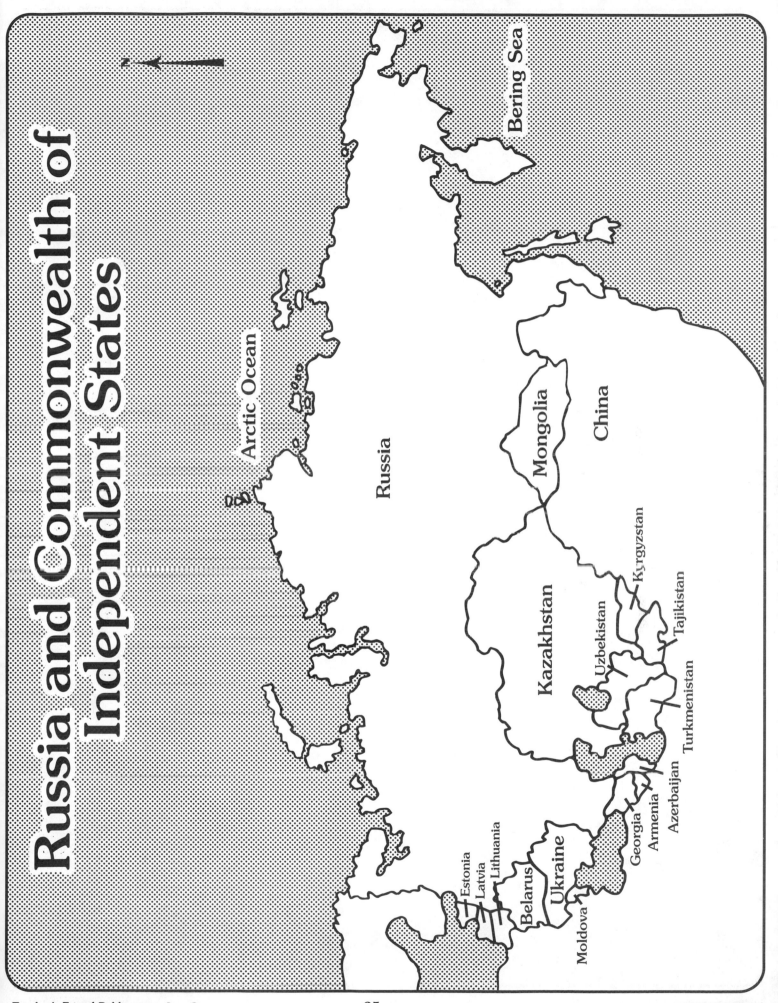

Bering Sea

Arctic Ocean

Russia

Mongolia

China

Kazakhstan

Uzbekistan

Kyrgyzstan

Tajikistan

Turkmenistan

Georgia

Armenia

Azerbaijan

Estonia

Latvia

Lithuania

Belarus

Ukraine

Moldova

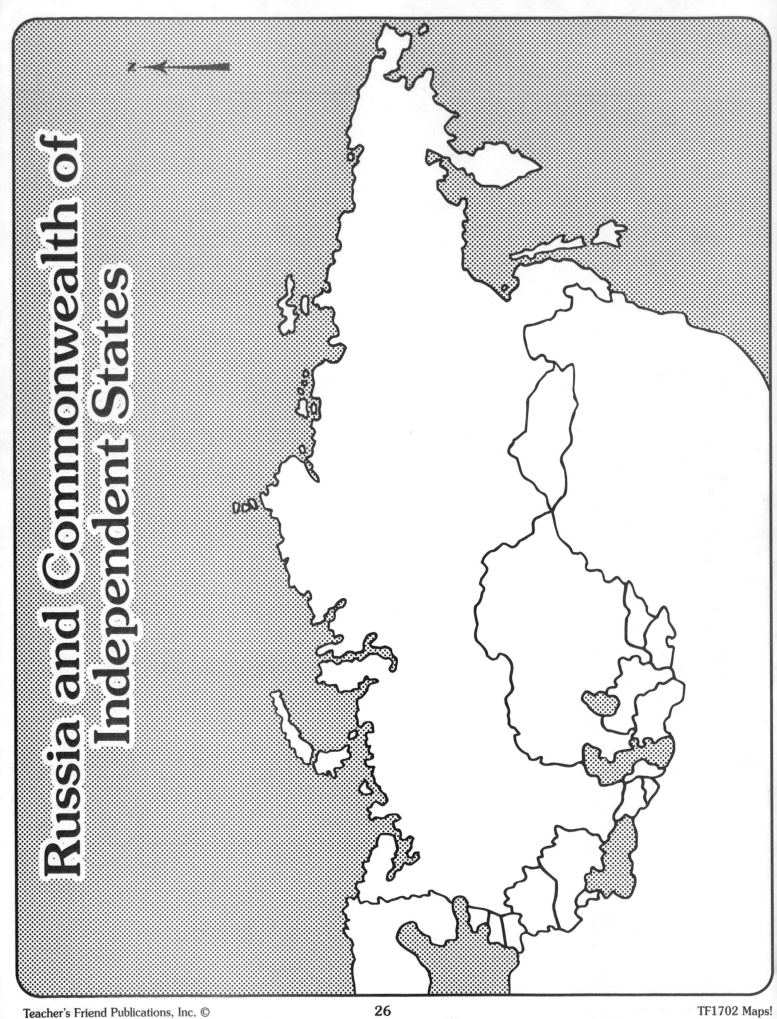

Russia and Commonwealth of Independent States

Antarctica

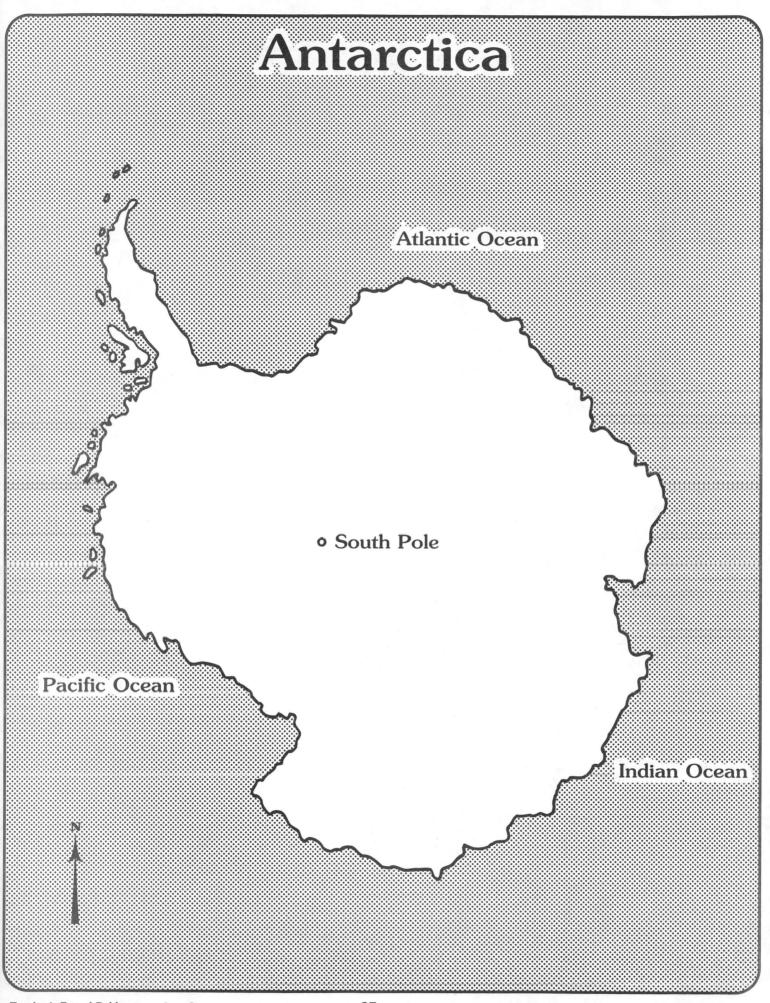

Atlantic Ocean

Pacific Ocean

o South Pole

Indian Ocean

N

Antarctica

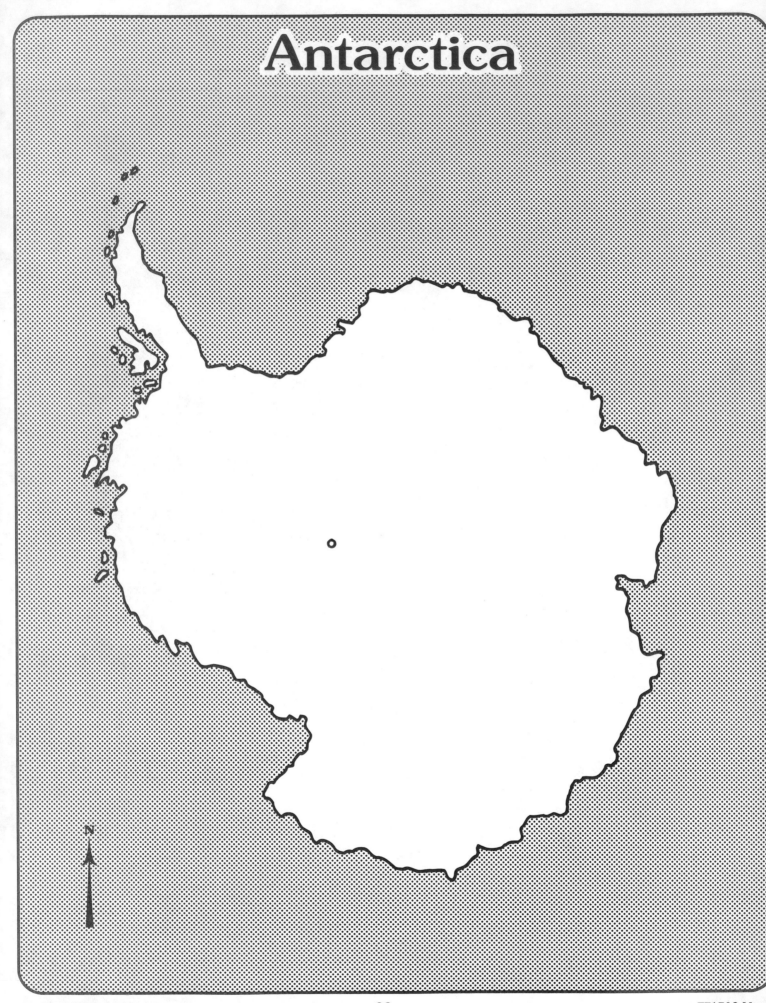

Caribbean Sea

West Indies

Venezuela

Guyana
Suriname

French Guiana

Colombia

Atlantic Ocean

Ecuador

Peru

Brazil

Bolivia

Pacific Ocean

Paraguay

Argentina

Chile

Uruguay

South America

Falkland Islands

Cape Horn

N

South America

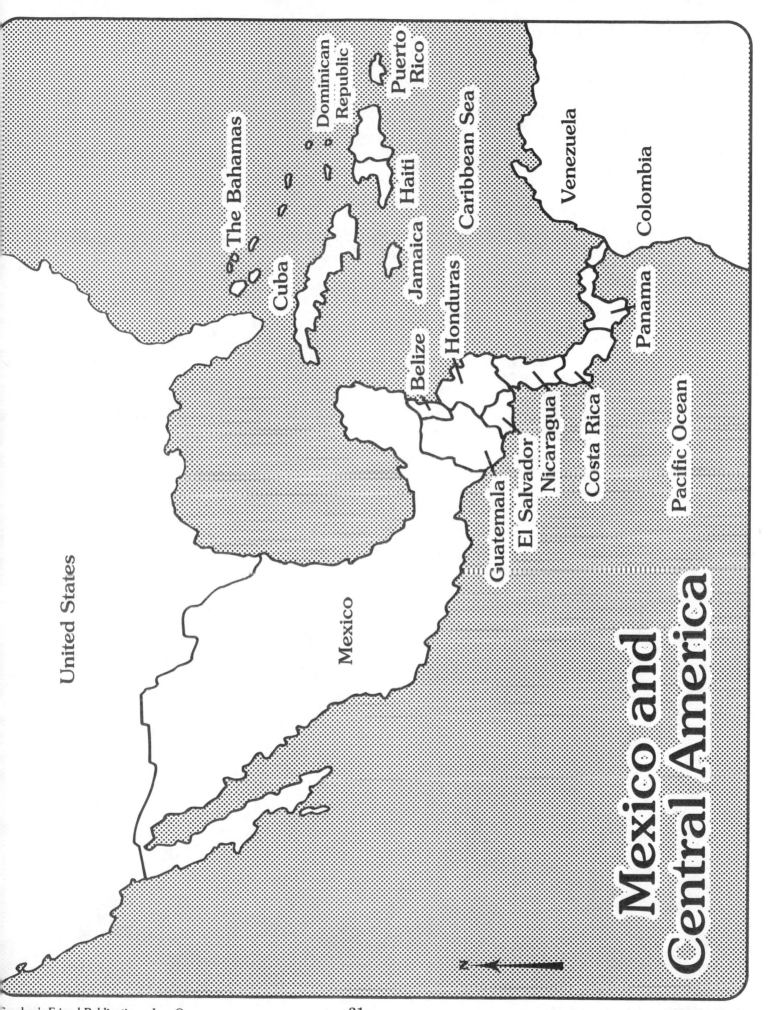

Mexico and Central America

United States

Mexico

The Bahamas

Cuba

Dominican Republic

Puerto Rico

Haiti

Jamaica

Caribbean Sea

Venezuela

Colombia

Belize

Honduras

Guatemala

El Salvador

Nicaragua

Costa Rica

Panama

Pacific Ocean

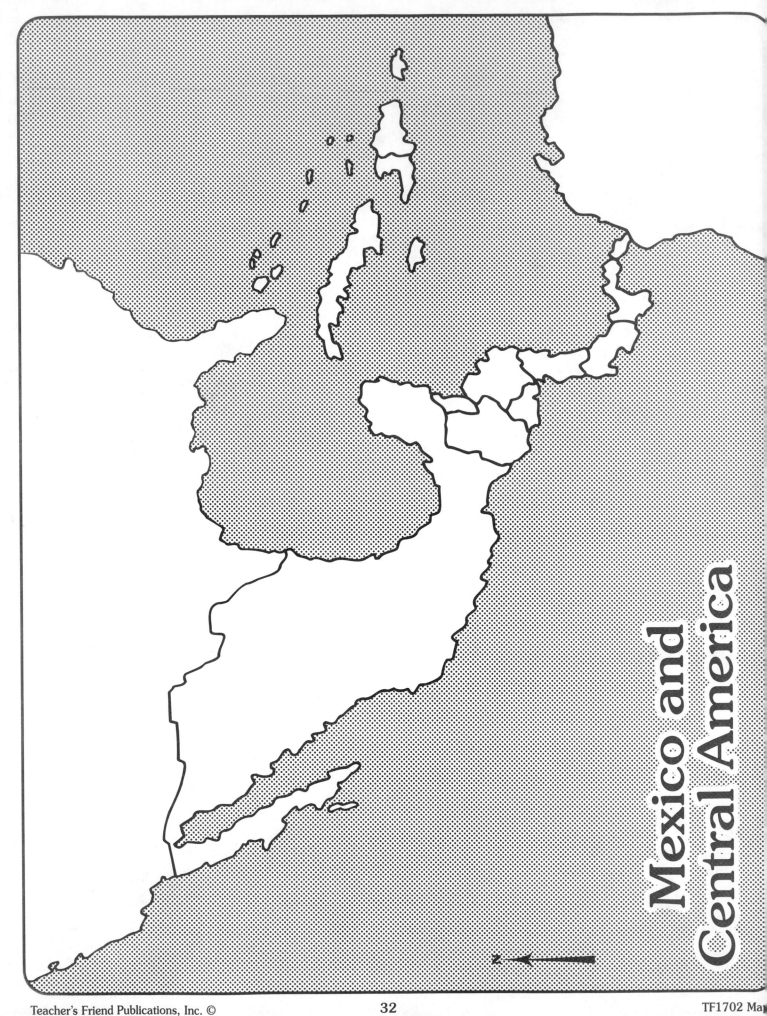

Mexico and Central America

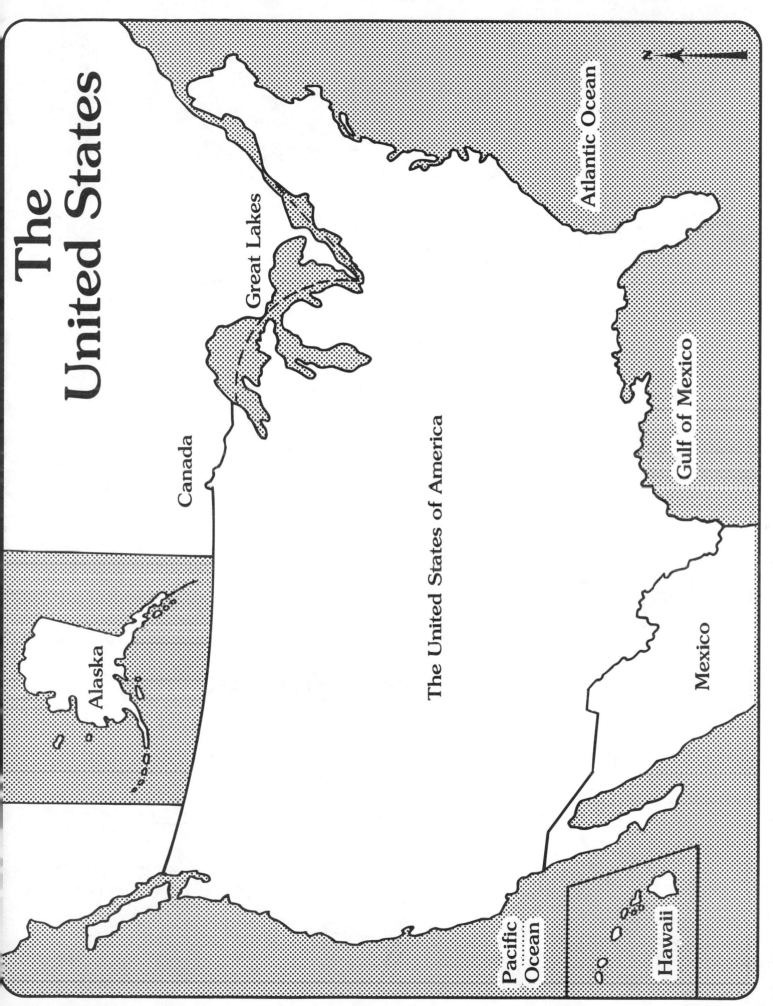

The United States

Canada

Great Lakes

Atlantic Ocean

Gulf of Mexico

The United States of America

Alaska

Mexico

Pacific Ocean

Hawaii

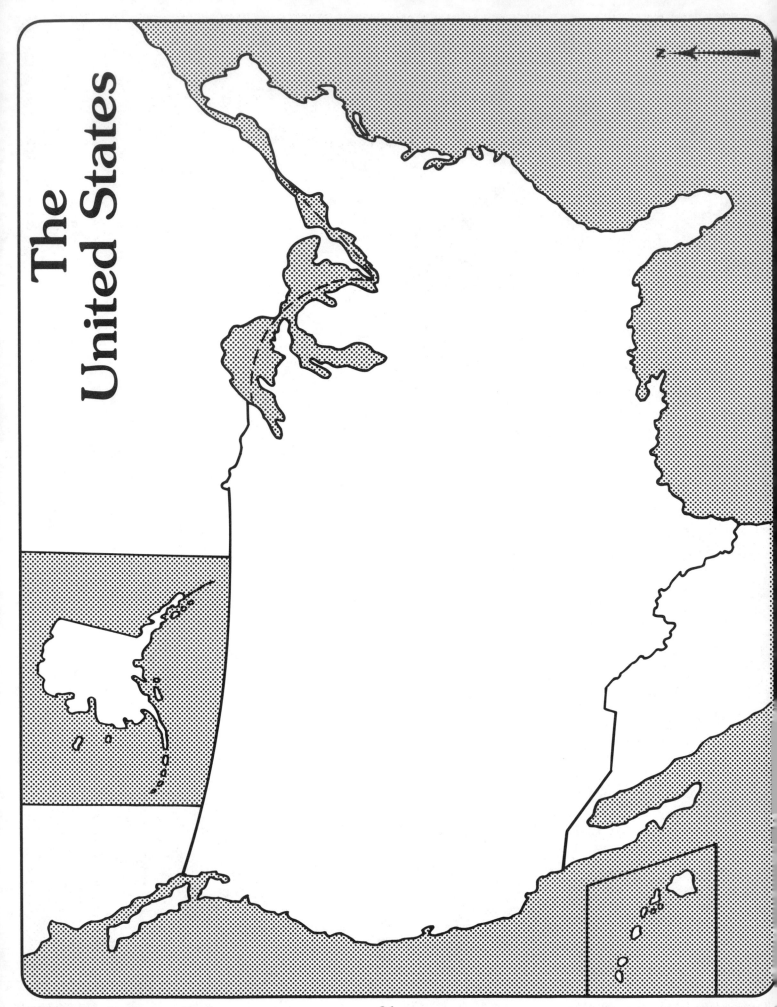

The United States

Canada

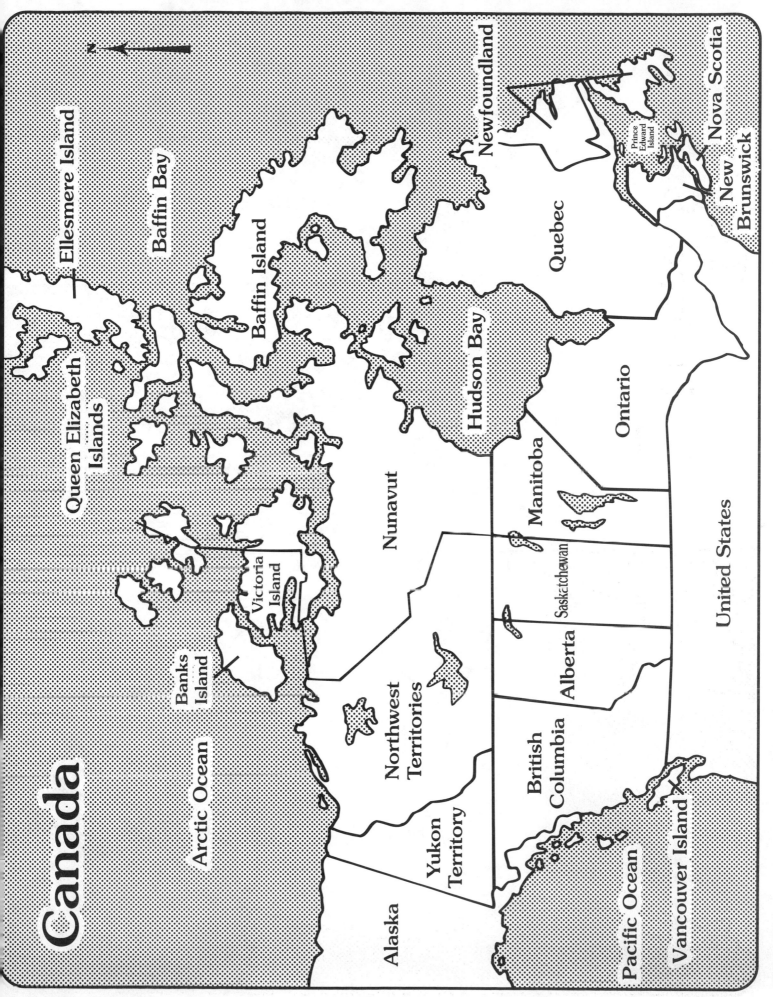

Ellesmere Island

Baffin Bay

Queen Elizabeth Islands

Baffin Island

Newfoundland

Prince Edward Island

Nova Scotia

New Brunswick

Quebec

Hudson Bay

Ontario

Victoria Island

Nunavut

Manitoba

Banks Island

Saskatchewan

United States

Arctic Ocean

Northwest Territories

Alberta

British Columbia

Yukon Territory

Alaska

Pacific Ocean

Vancouver Island

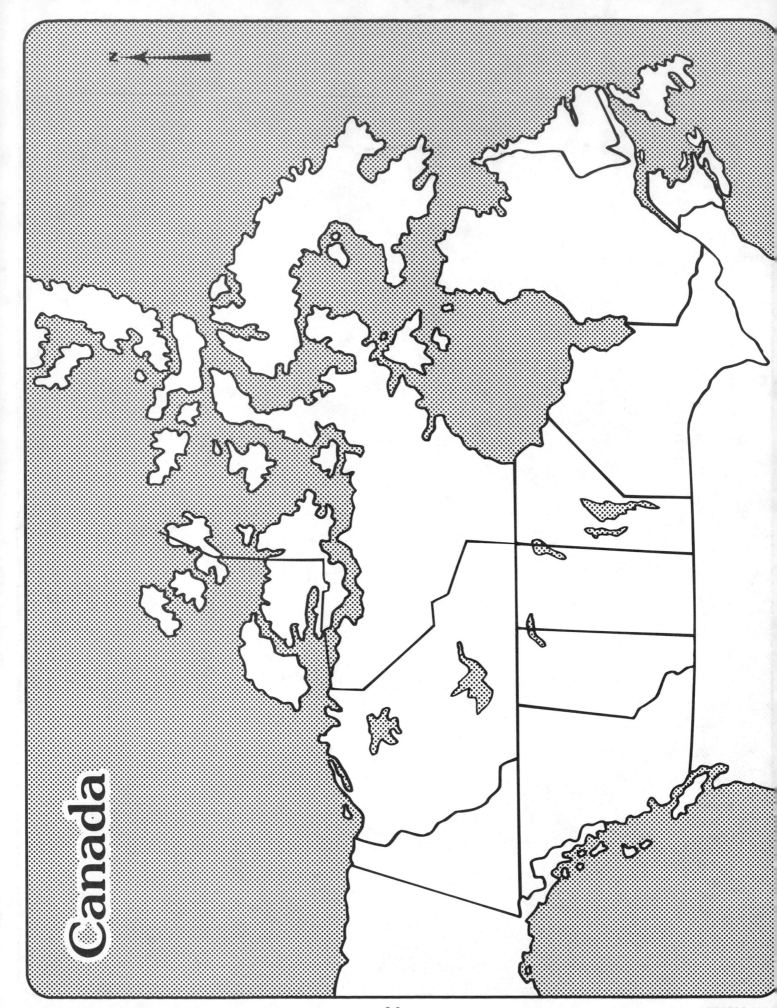

Canada

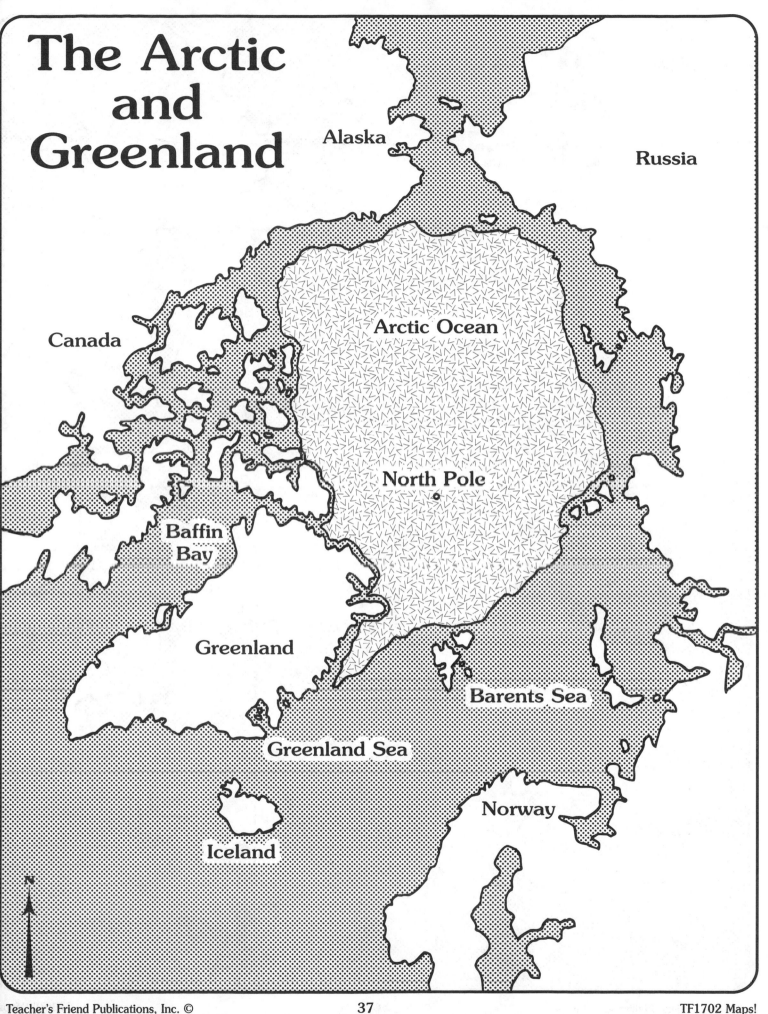

The Arctic and Greenland

Alaska

Russia

Canada

Arctic Ocean

North Pole

Baffin Bay

Greenland

Barents Sea

Greenland Sea

Norway

Iceland

N

The Arctic and Greenland

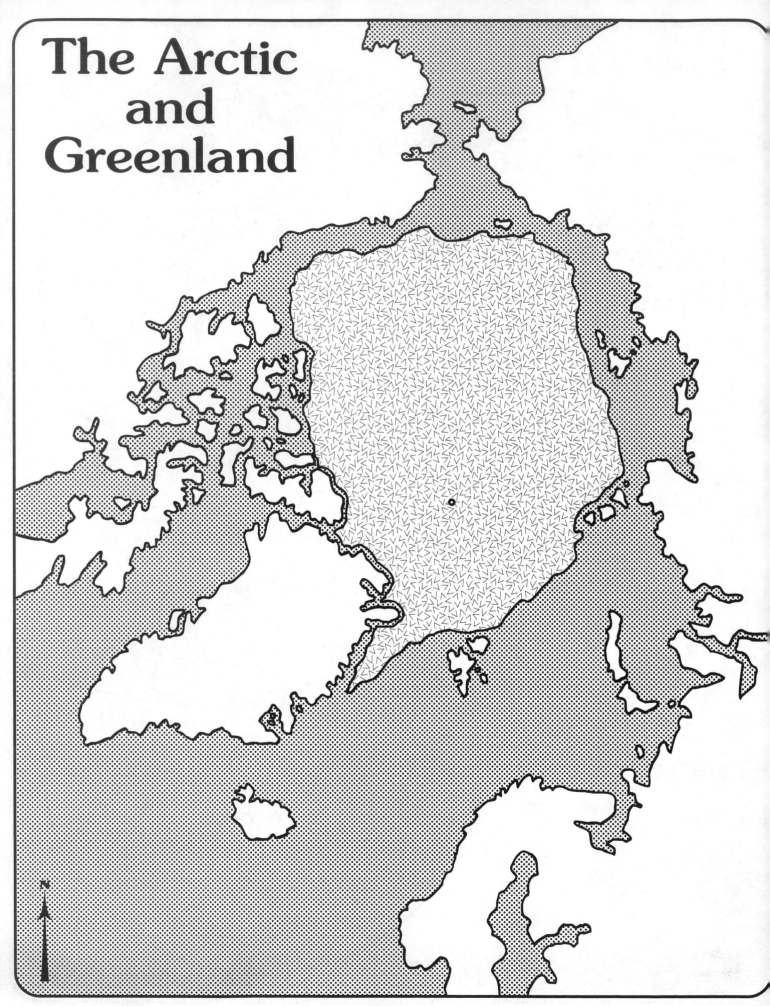

The Western Hemisphere

The Eastern Hemisphere

NAME: _____ DATE: _____

MY COUNTRY REPORT!

Name of Country: _____

Capital City: _____

Government: _____

Language(s): _____

Population: _____

Currency: _____

Main Industries: _____

_____

_____

_____

The Flag of: _____

Important Dates and Events:

_____ _____

_____

_____ _____

_____

_____ _____

_____

_____ _____

_____

The United States

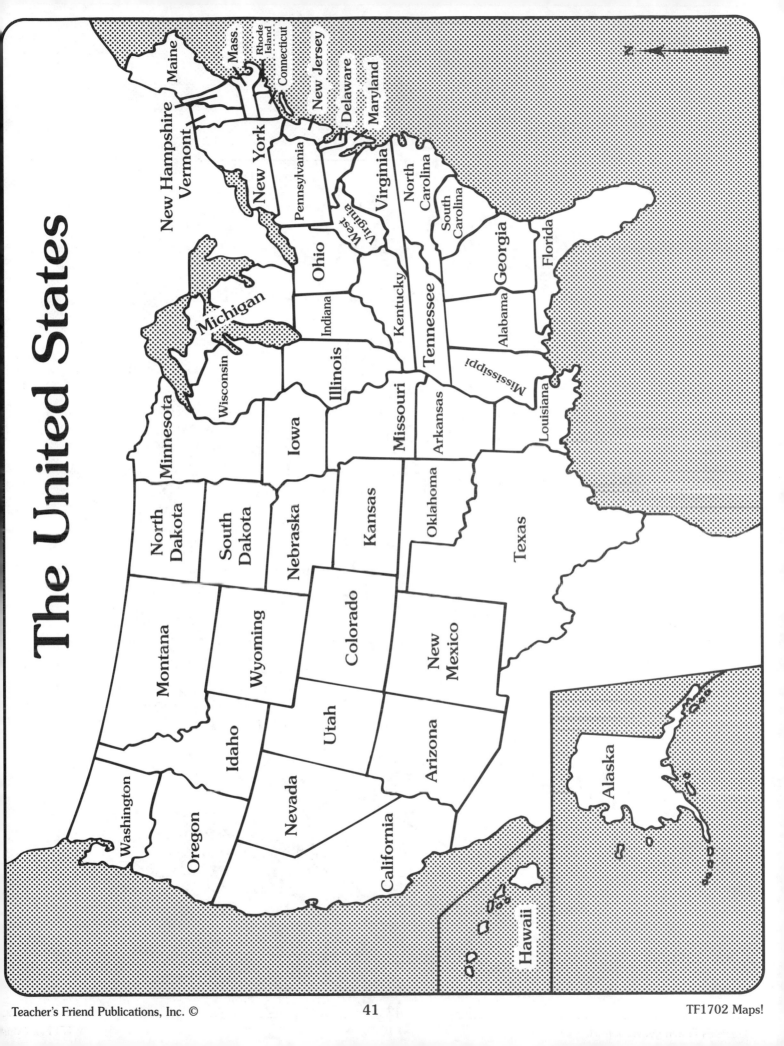

The United States

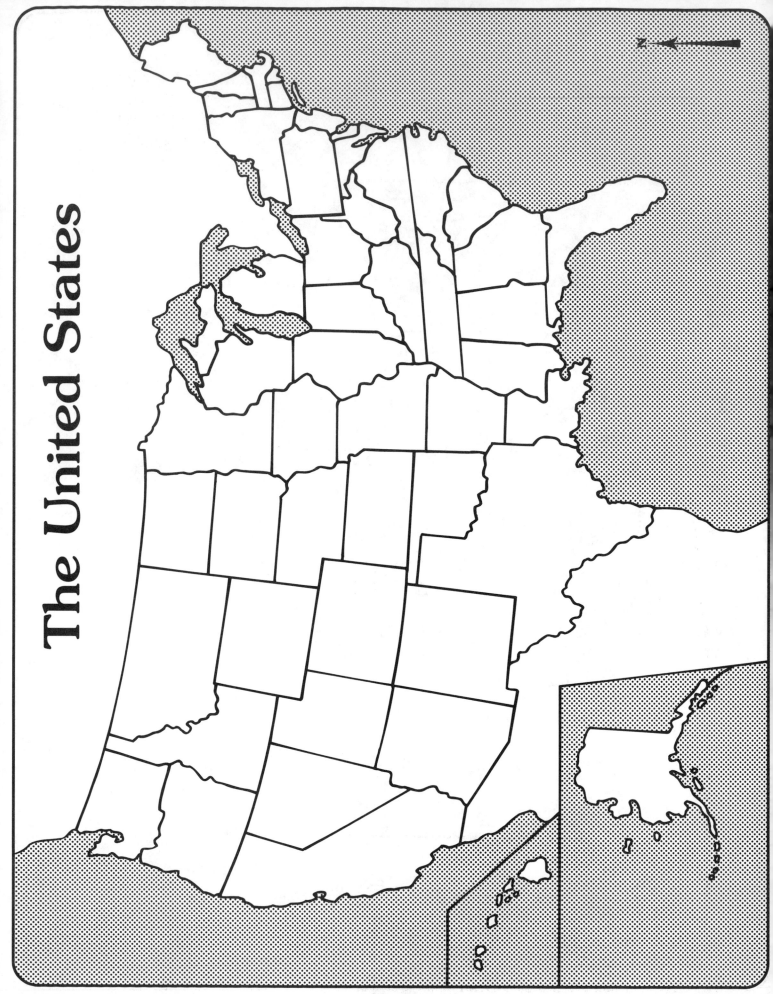

Alabama

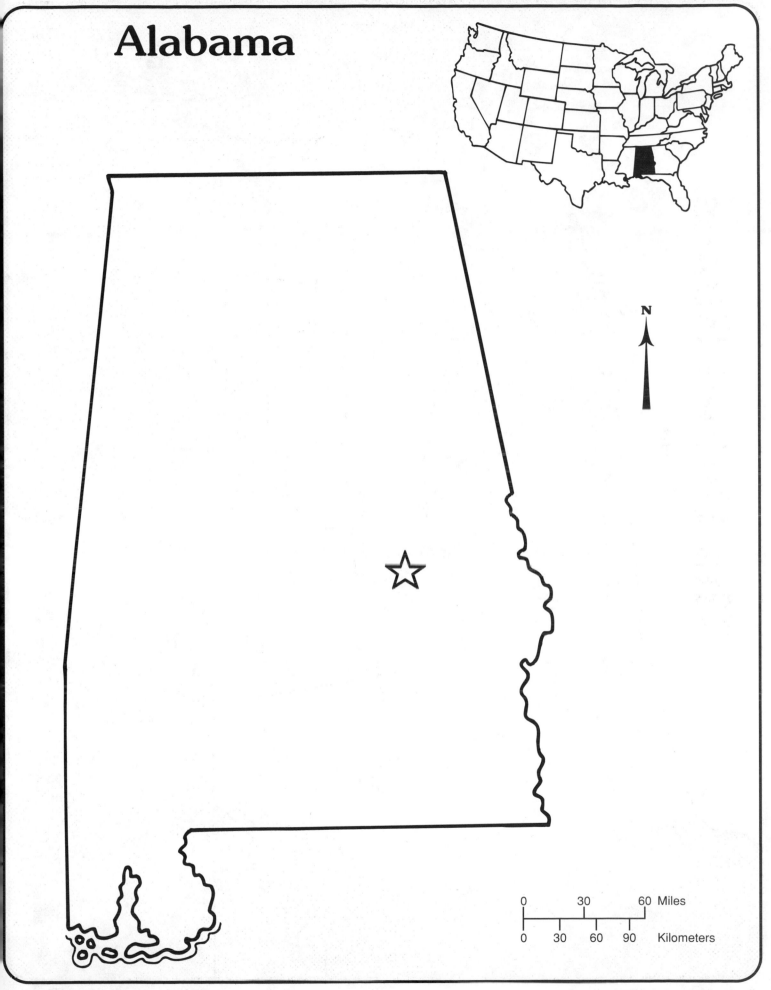

0   30   60 Miles

0   30   60   90   Kilometers

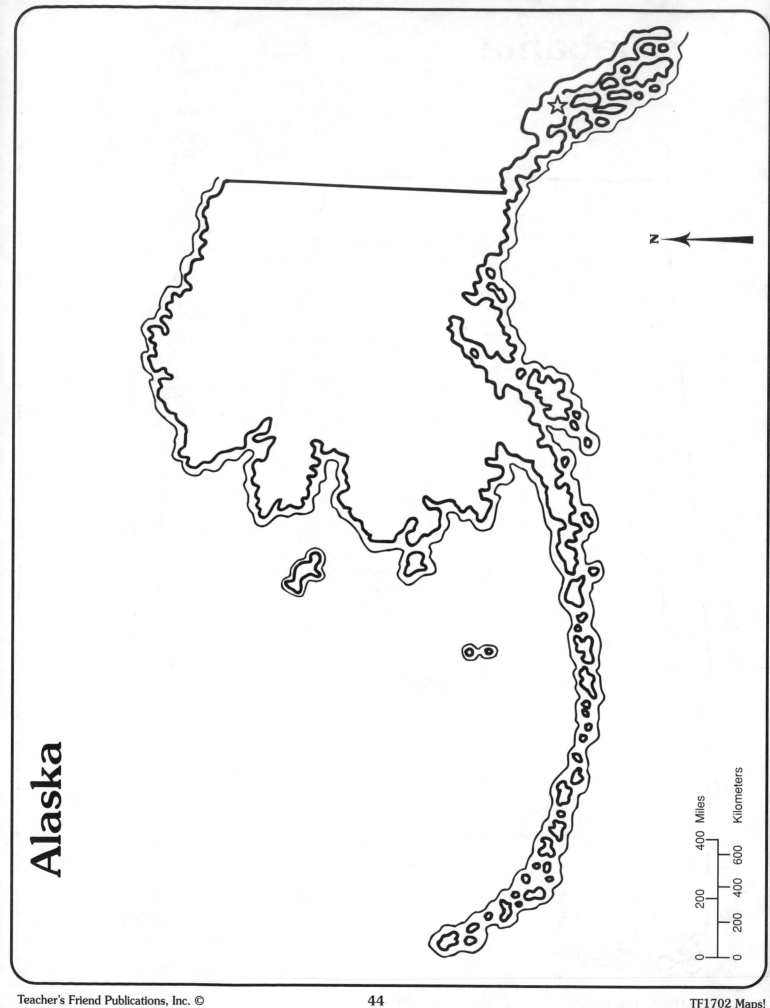

Alaska

N

Miles
400

Kilometers
600
400
400
200
200
200
0
0

Arizona

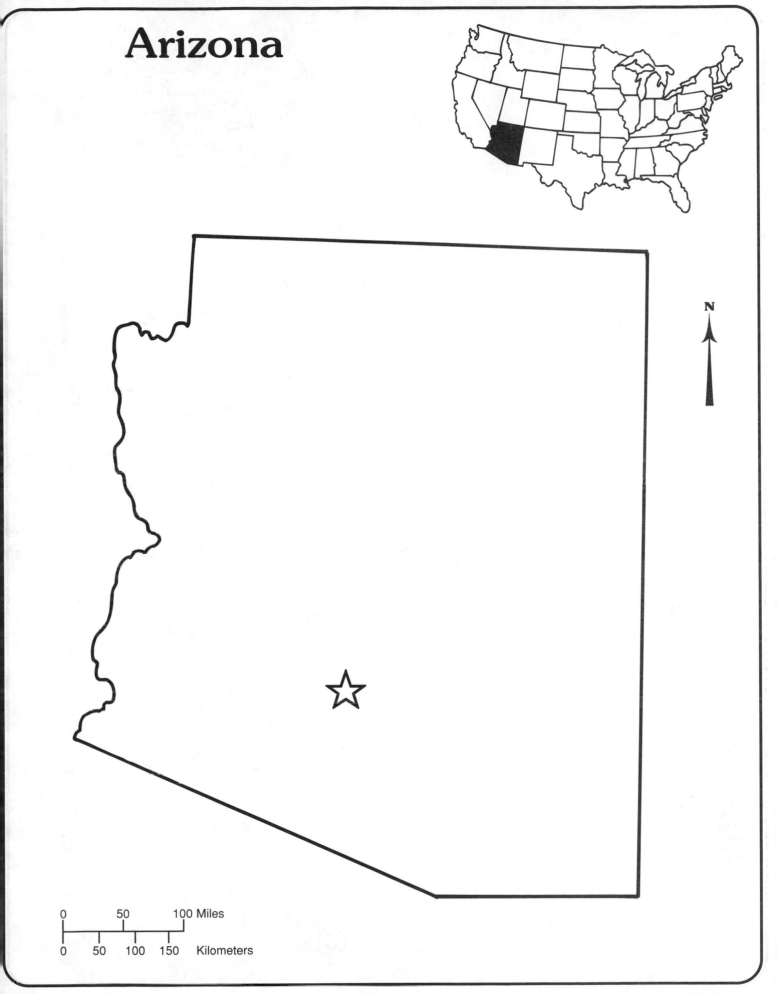

N

0   50   100 Miles

0   50 100 150   Kilometers

Ararkansas

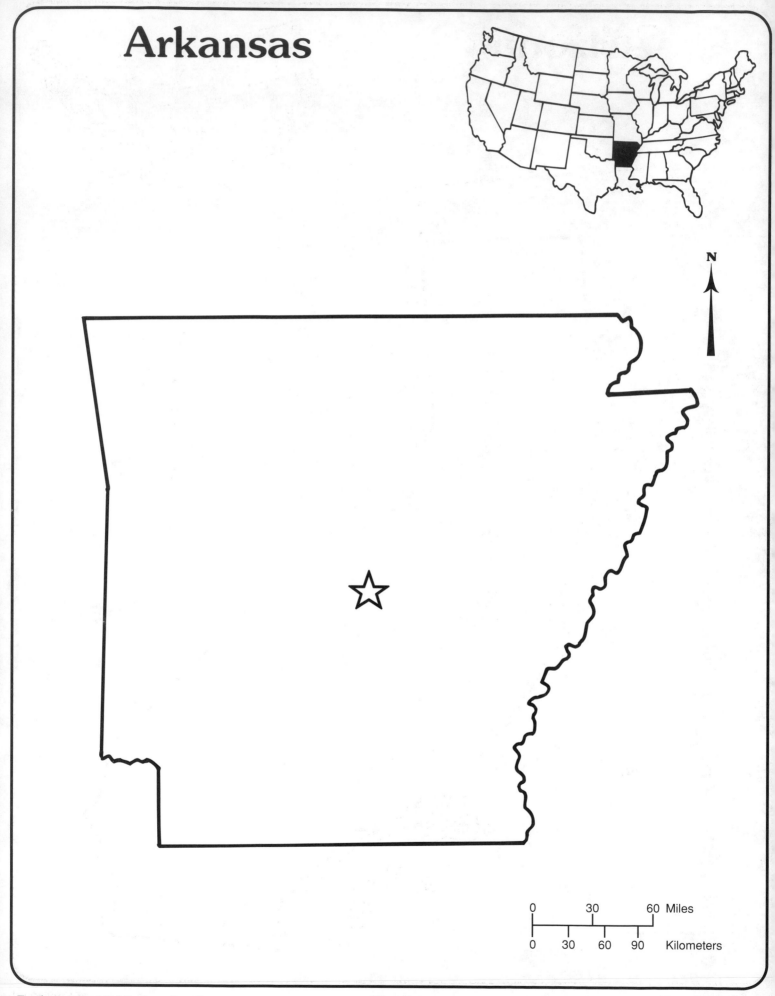

N

0   30   60 Miles

0   30   60   90 Kilometers

California

0   50   100 Miles

0   50   100   150   Kilometers

Colorado

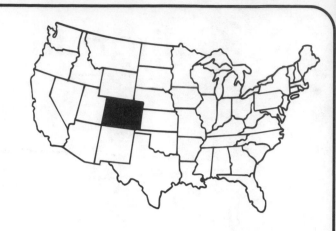

N

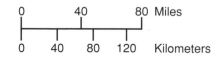

| 0 | | 40 | | 80 Miles |
| 0 | 40 | 80 | 120 | Kilometers |

Connecticut

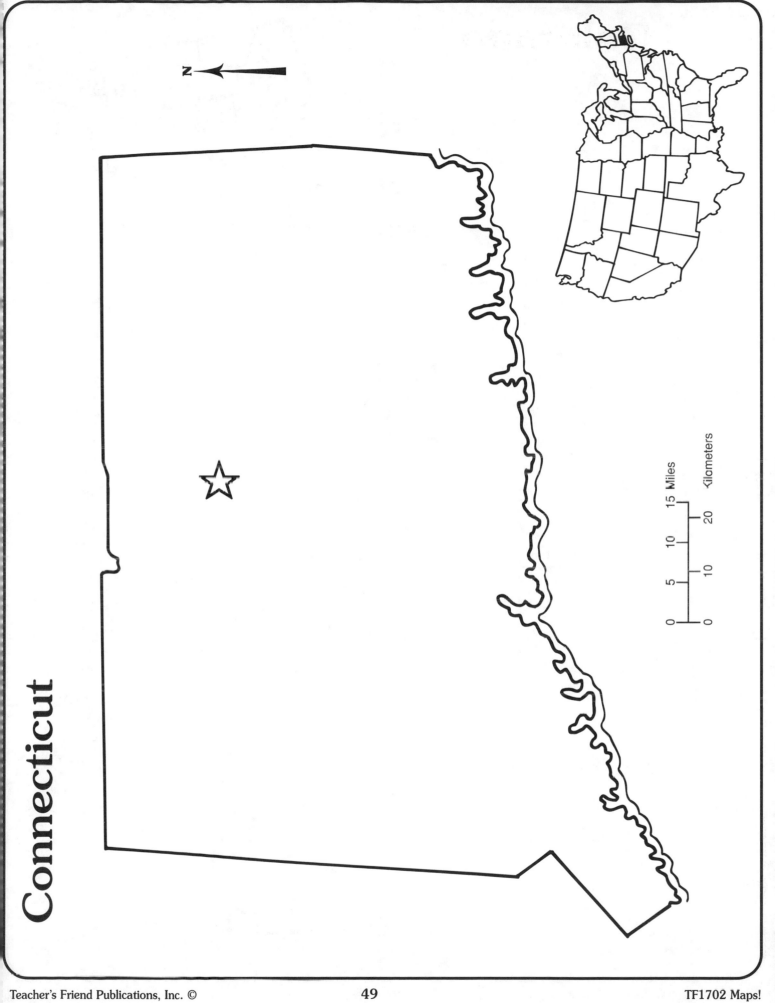

N

15 Miles

Kilometers

Delaware

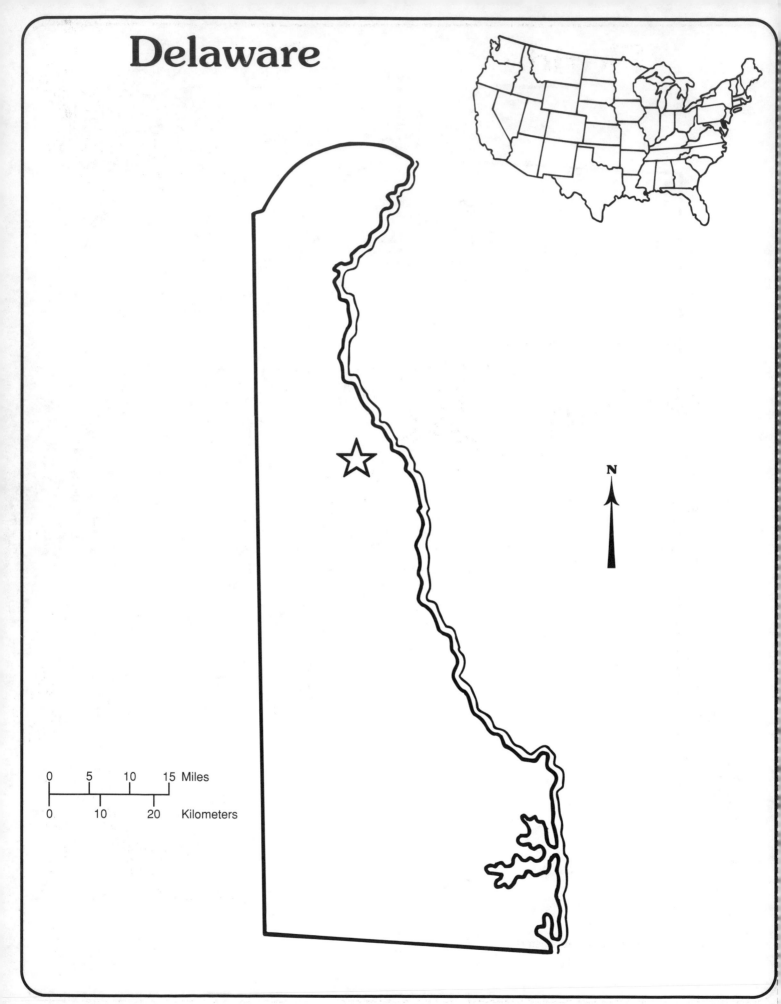

0   5   10   15 Miles

0   10   20 Kilometers

N

Florida

0   50   100 Miles

0   50   100   150   Kilometers

Georgia

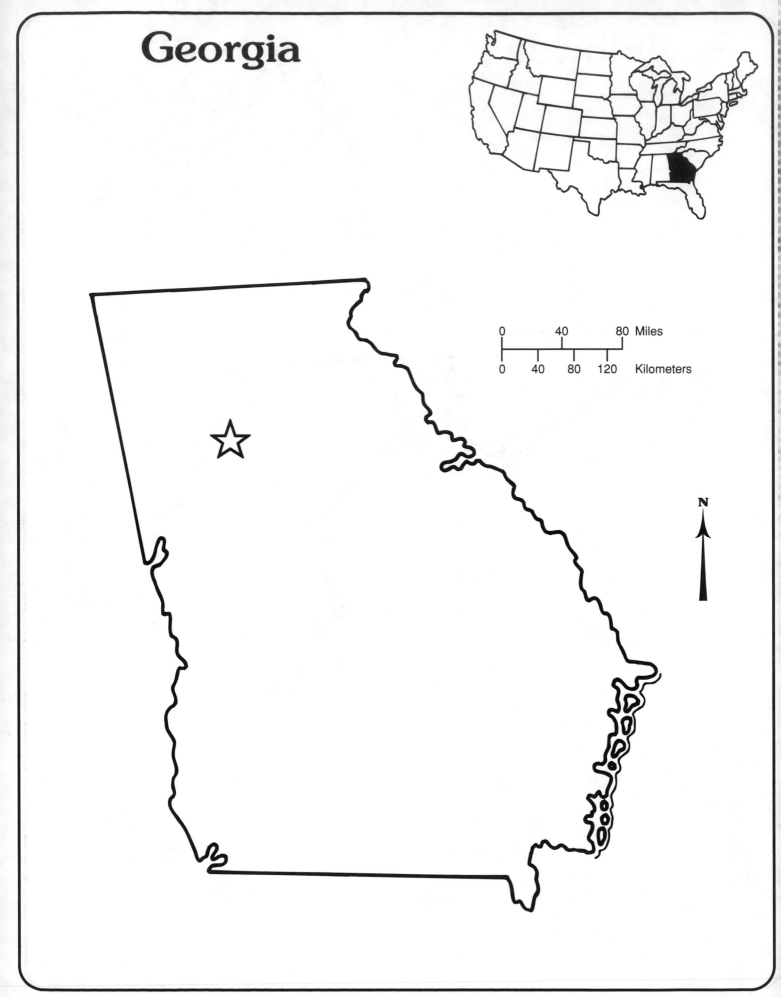

0   40   80 Miles

0   40   80   120 Kilometers

N

Hawaii

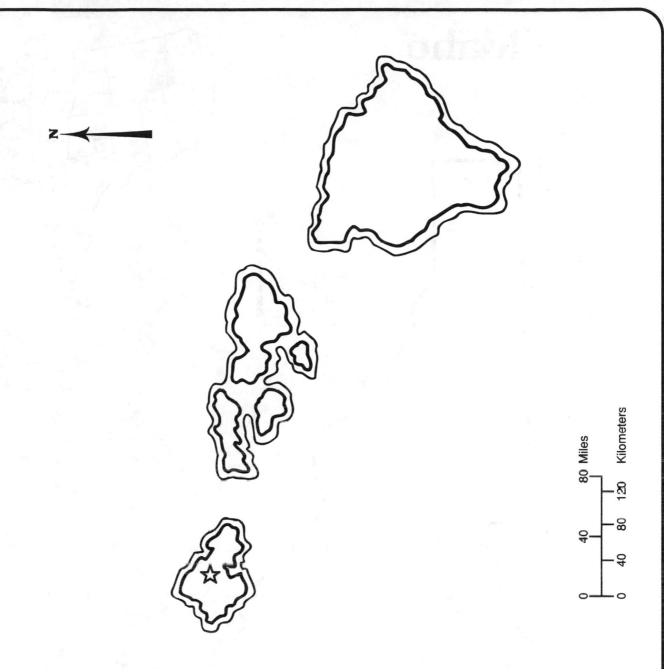

N ←

80 Miles

40   40

0   0

40   80   120

Kilometers

Idaho

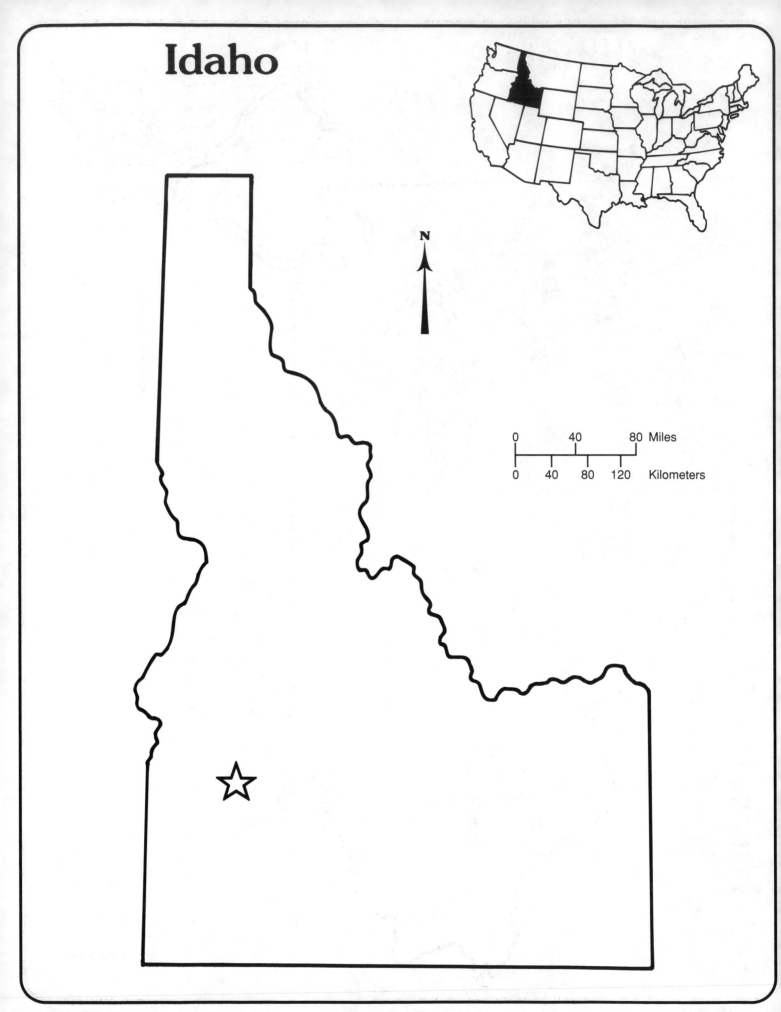

N

| 0 | | 40 | | 80 Miles |
| 0 | 40 | 80 | 120 | Kilometers |

Illinois

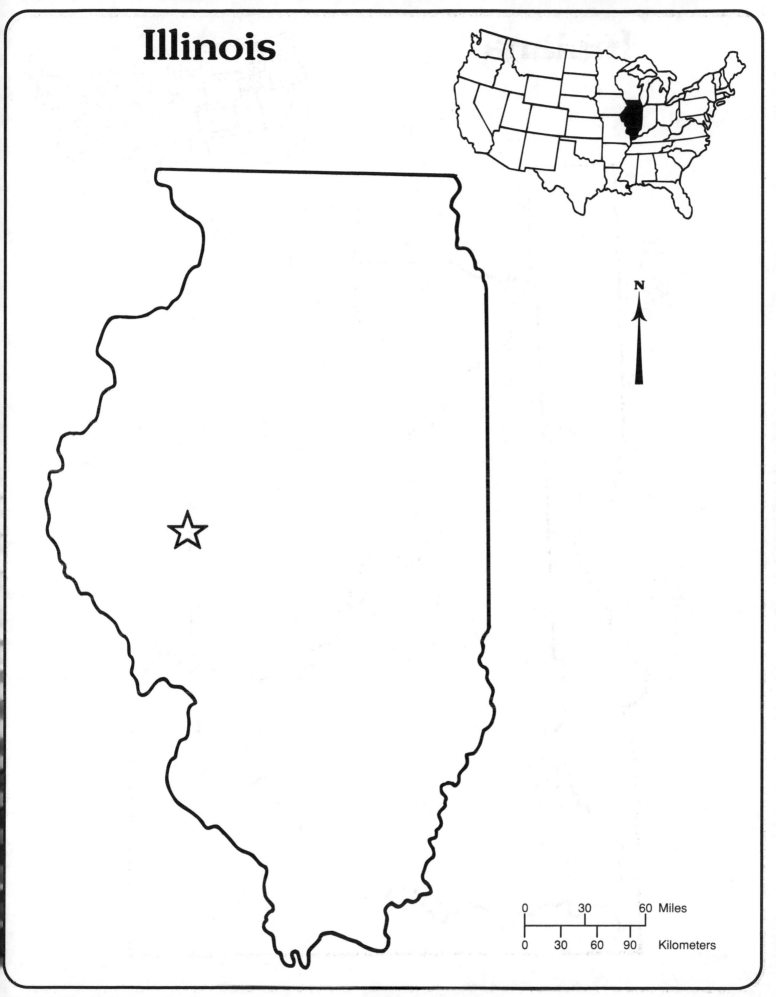

Indiana

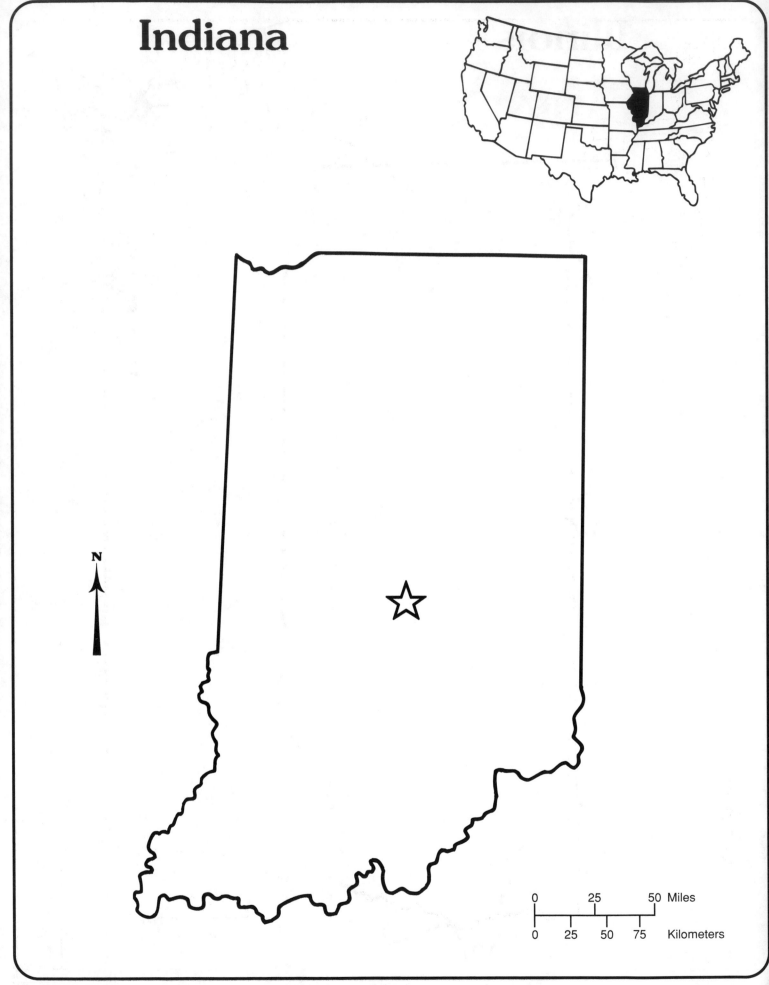

N

0   25   50 Miles

0   25   50   75   Kilometers

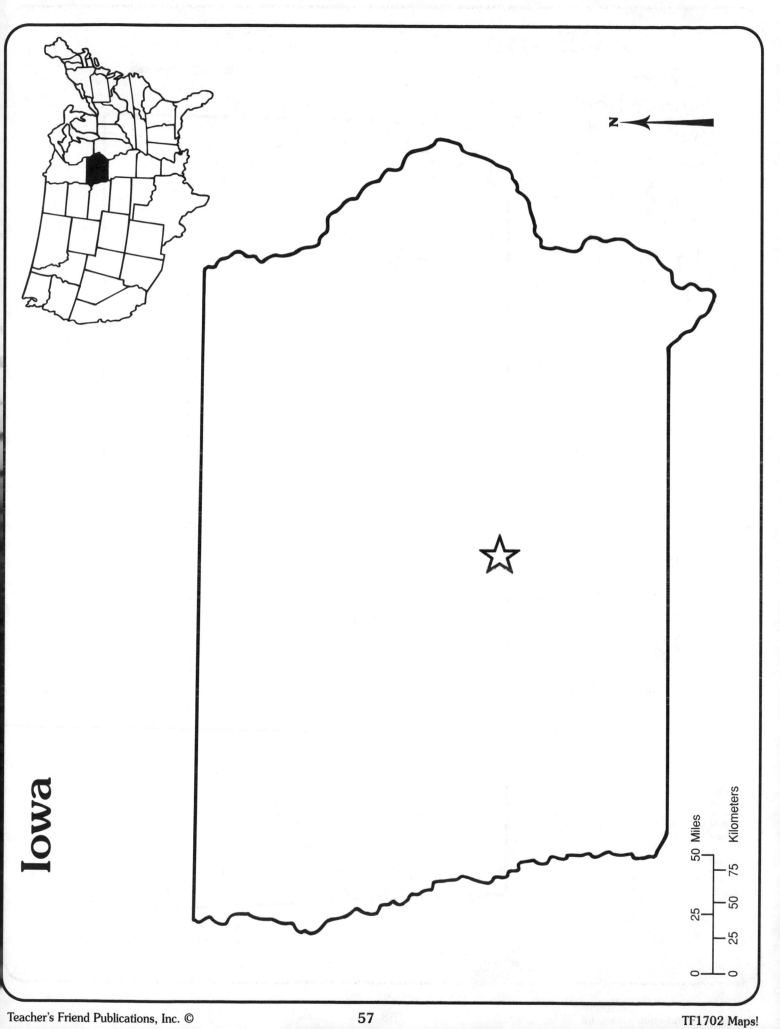

Iowa

N ←

50 Miles

Kilometers

50

75

25

50

25

25

0

0

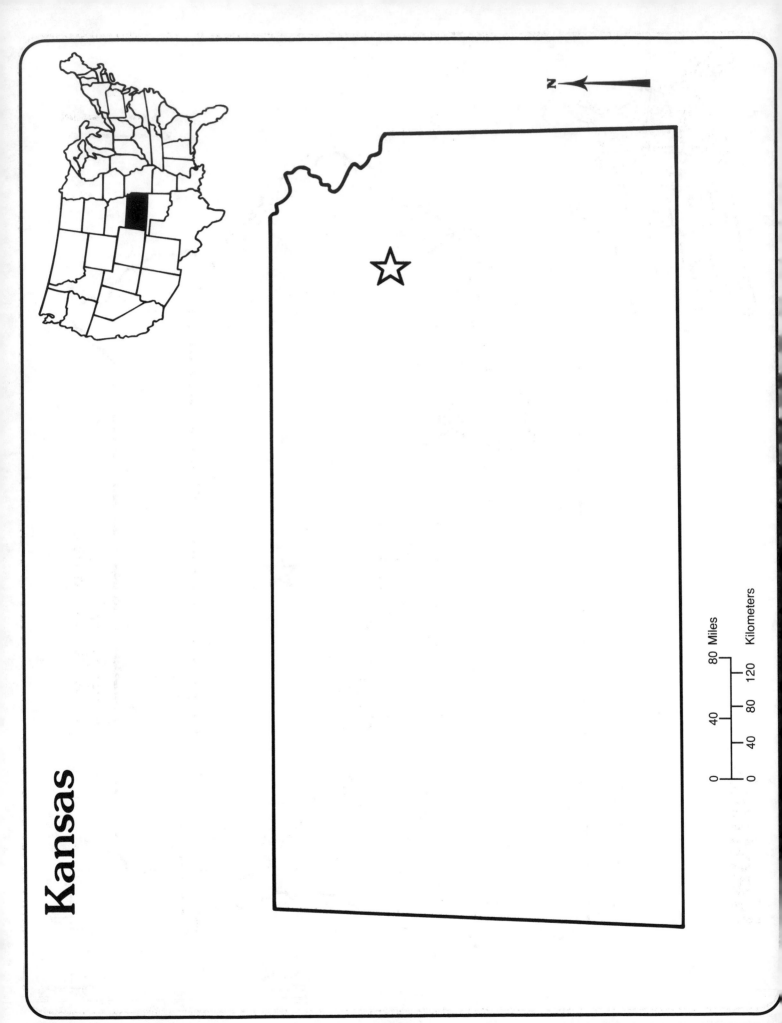

Kansas

N

0	40	80 Miles	
0	40	80	120 Kilometers

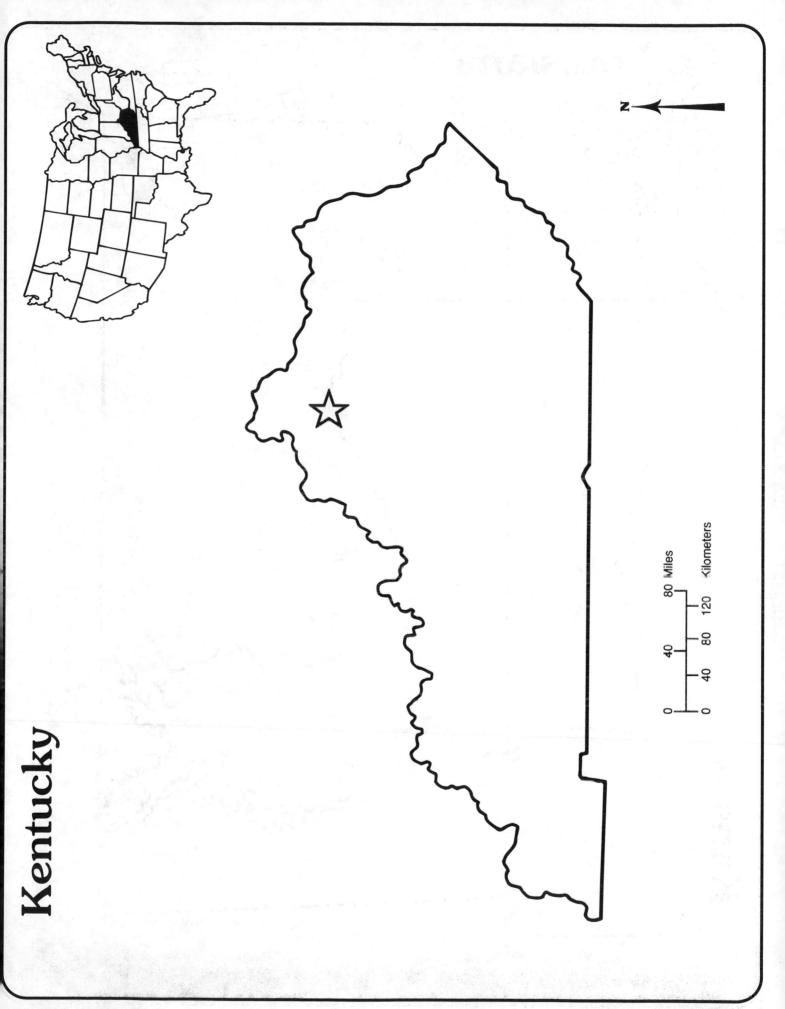

Kentucky

80 Miles
Kilometers

120
80
40
40
40

0   0

Louisiana

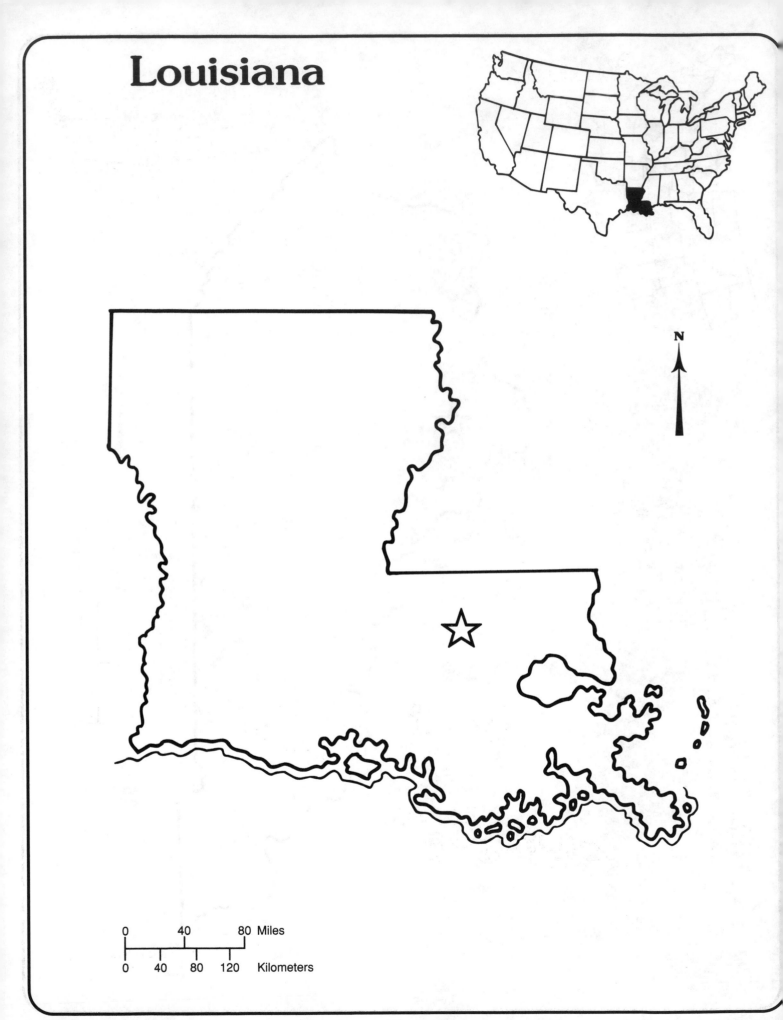

0   40   80 Miles

0   40   80   120   Kilometers

Maine

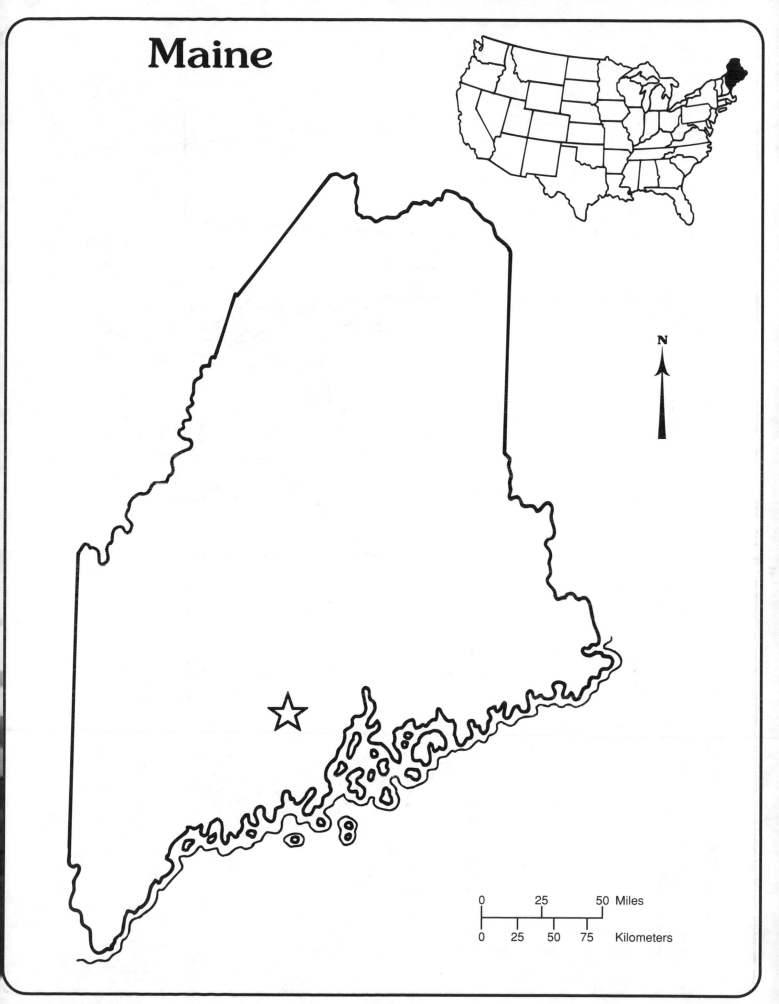

0   25   50 Miles

0   25   50   75 Kilometers

Maryland and Washington, D.C.

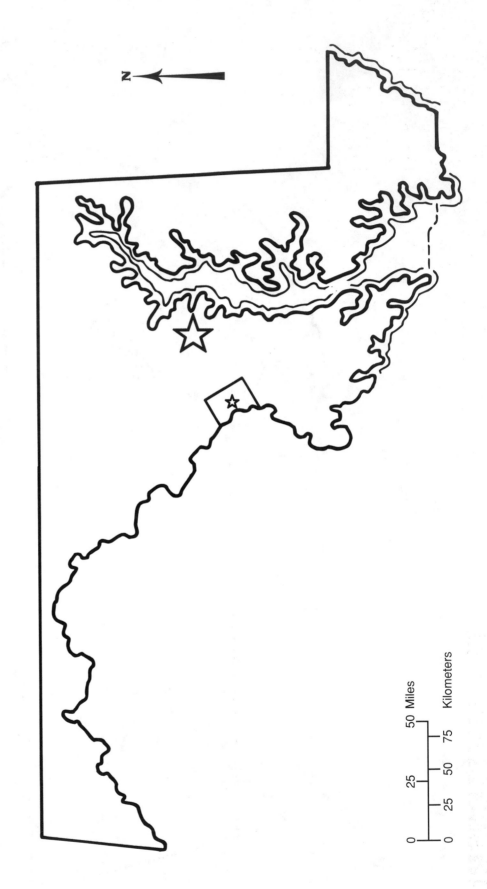

N

50 Miles

25

25

Kilometers

75

50

25

0

0

Massachusetts

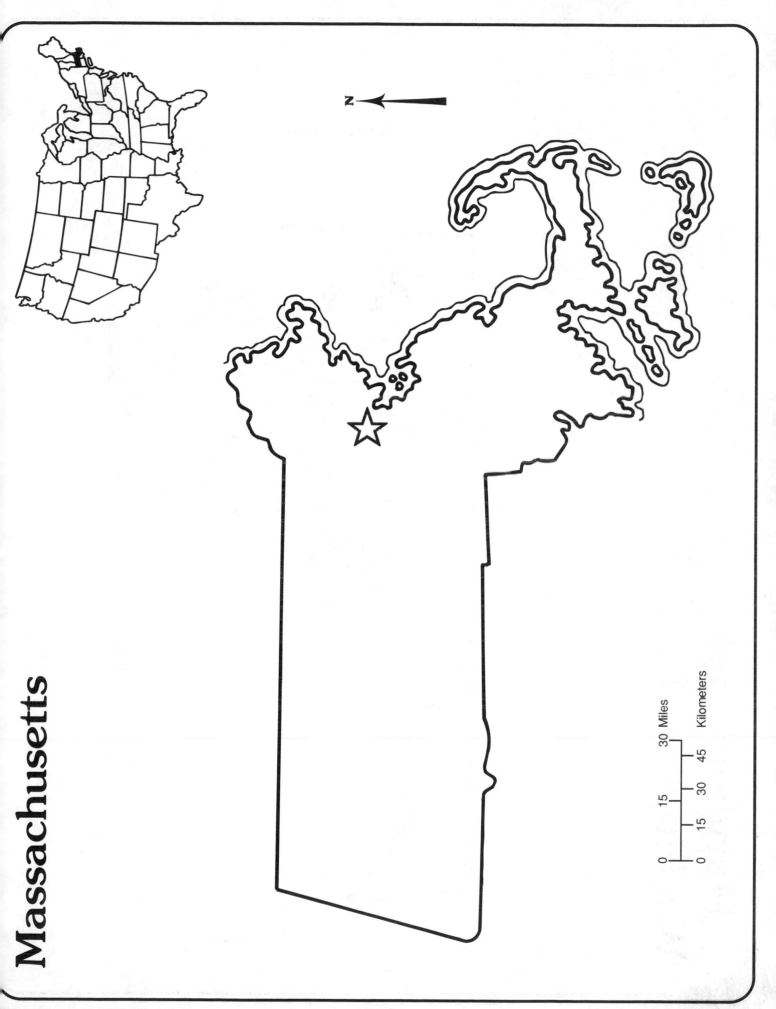

N

30 Miles   Kilometers

0   15   15   30   30   45

Michigan

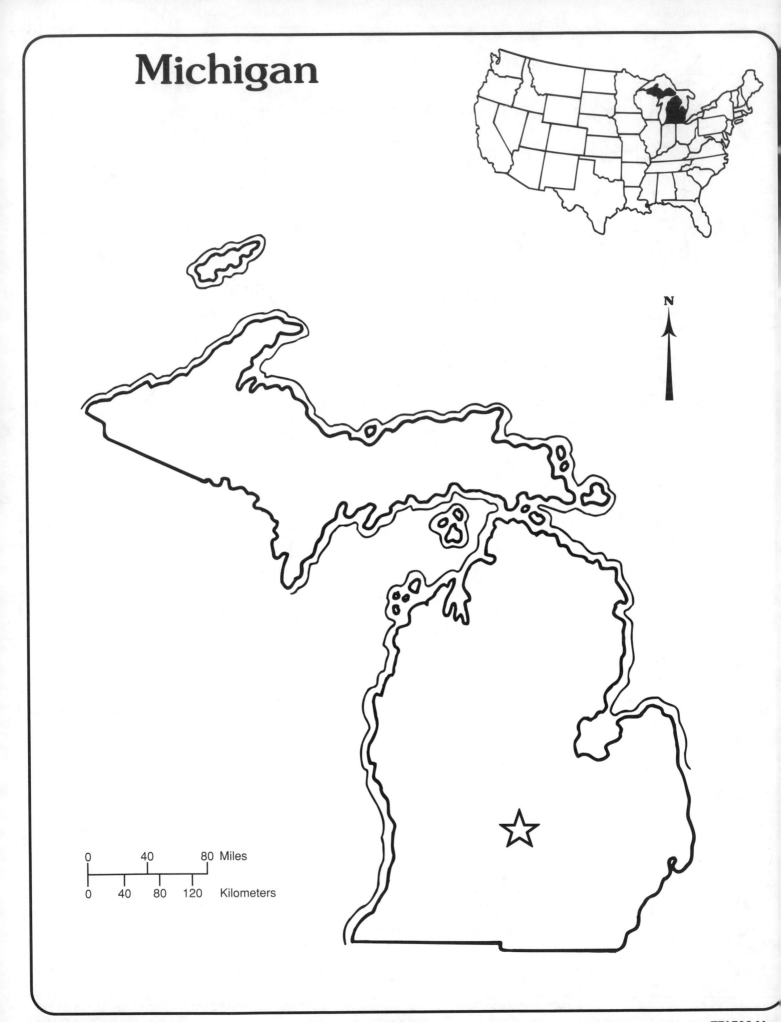

N

0   40   80 Miles

0   40 80 120 Kilometers

Minnesota

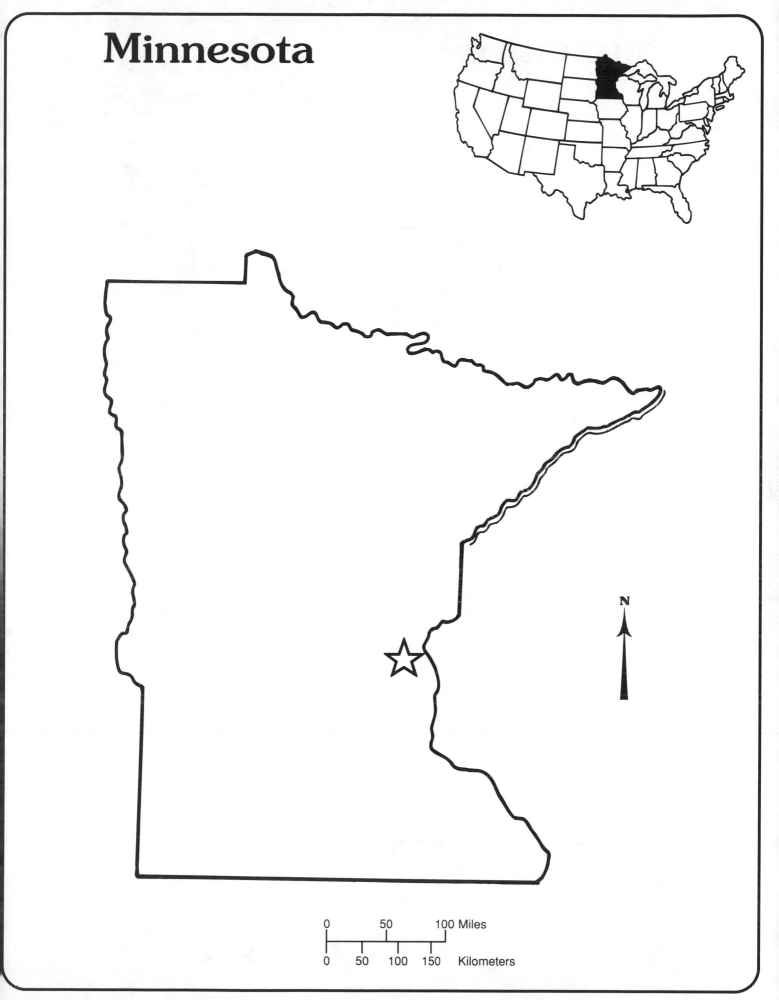

0   50   100 Miles

0   50   100   150   Kilometers

N

Mississippi

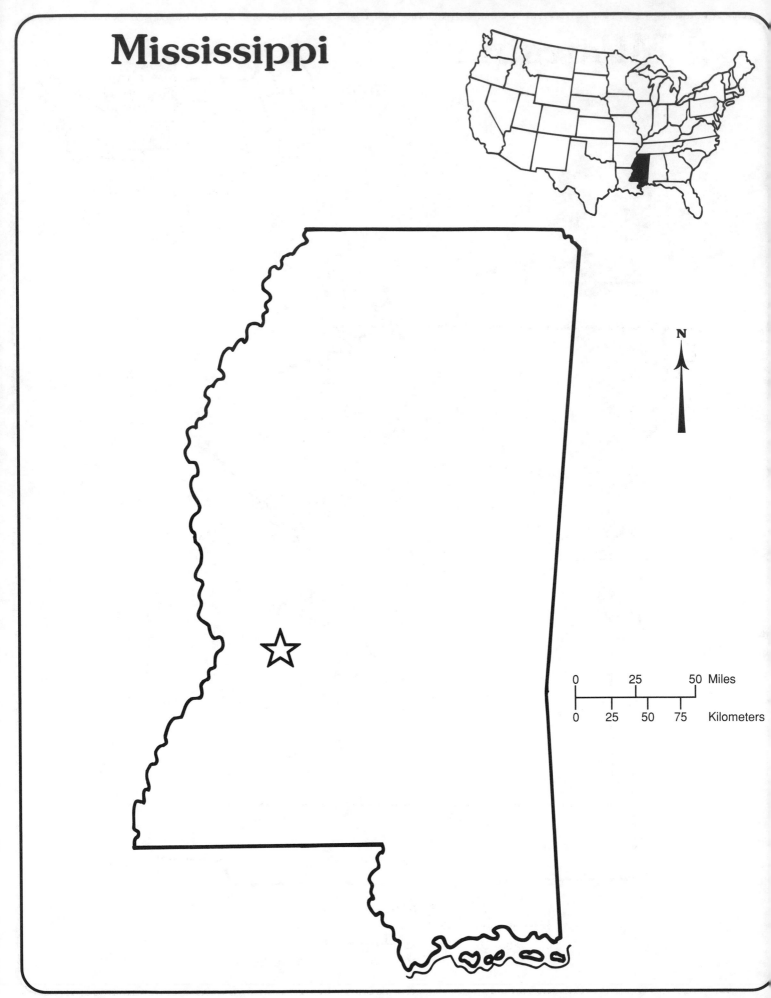

N

0   25   50 Miles

0   25   50   75 Kilometers

Missouri

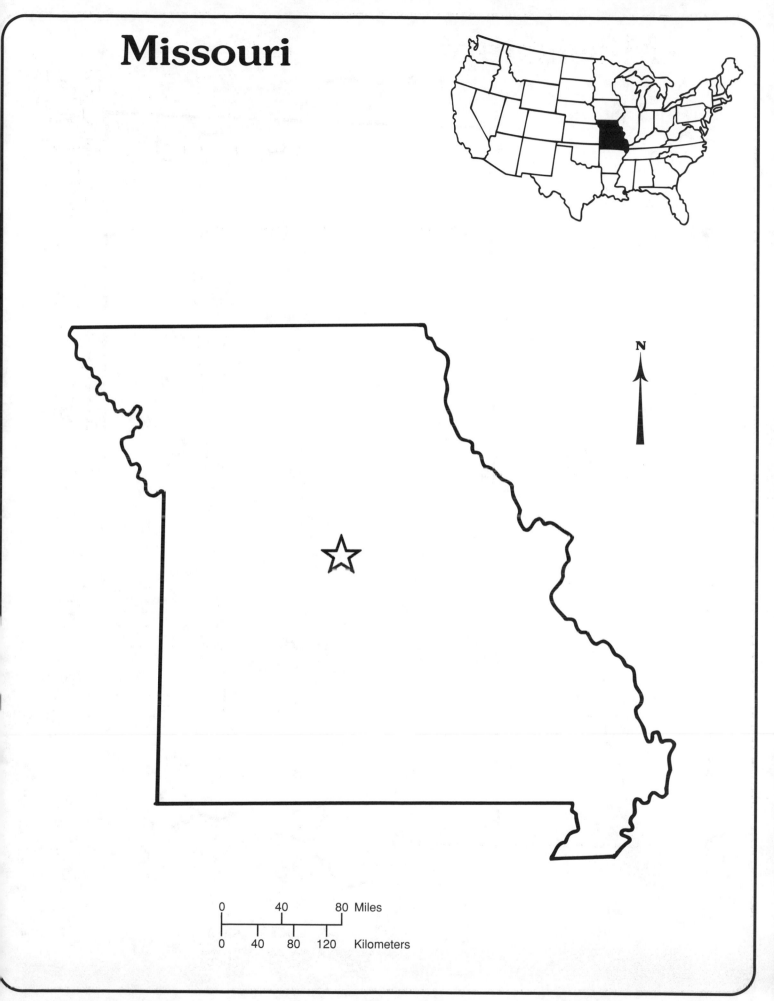

0   40   80 Miles

0   40   80   120   Kilometers

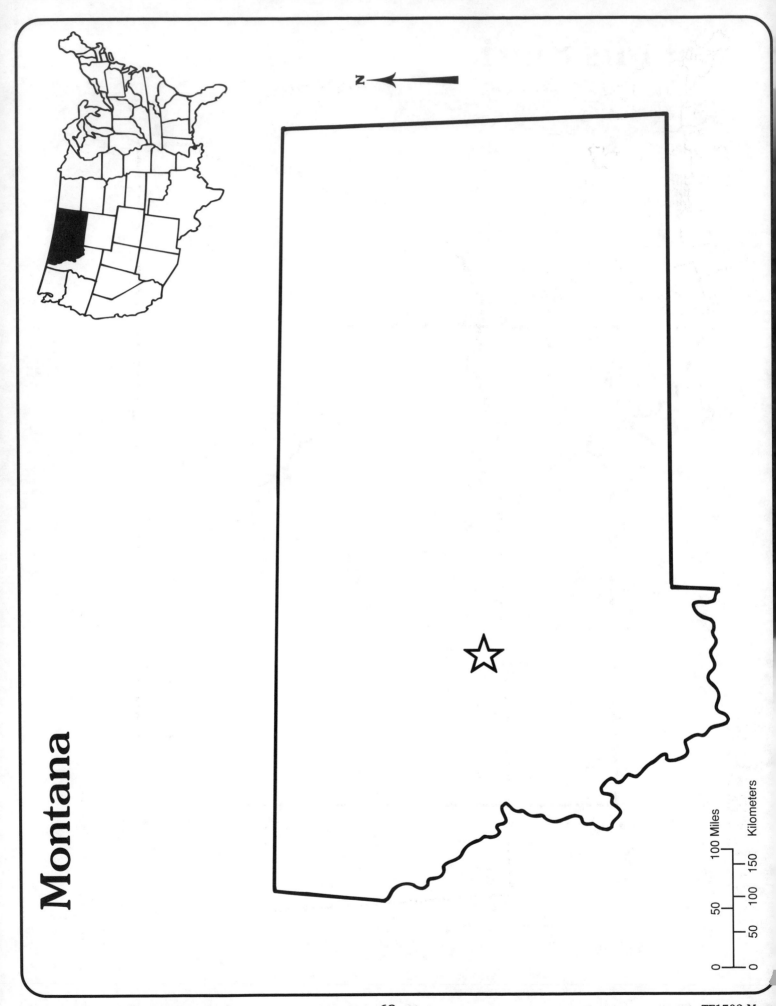

Montana

N

100 Miles

Kilometers

50   150

50   100

0   0

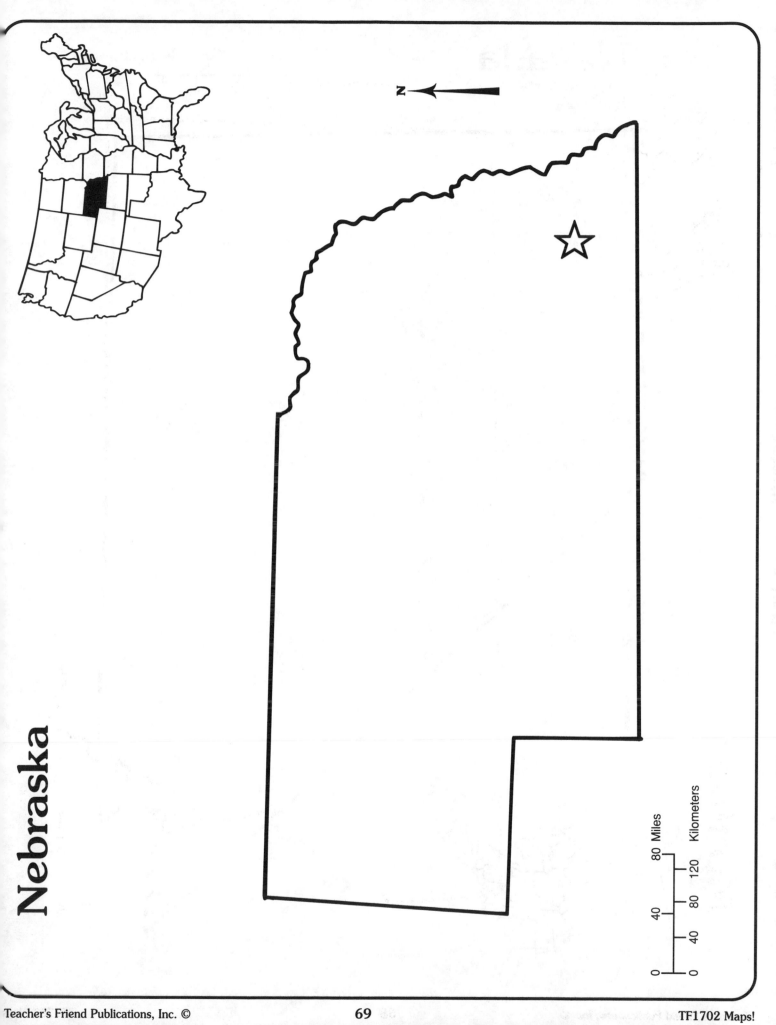

Nebraska

N ←

★

80 Miles

120

80

40 40

0 0

Kilometers

Nevada

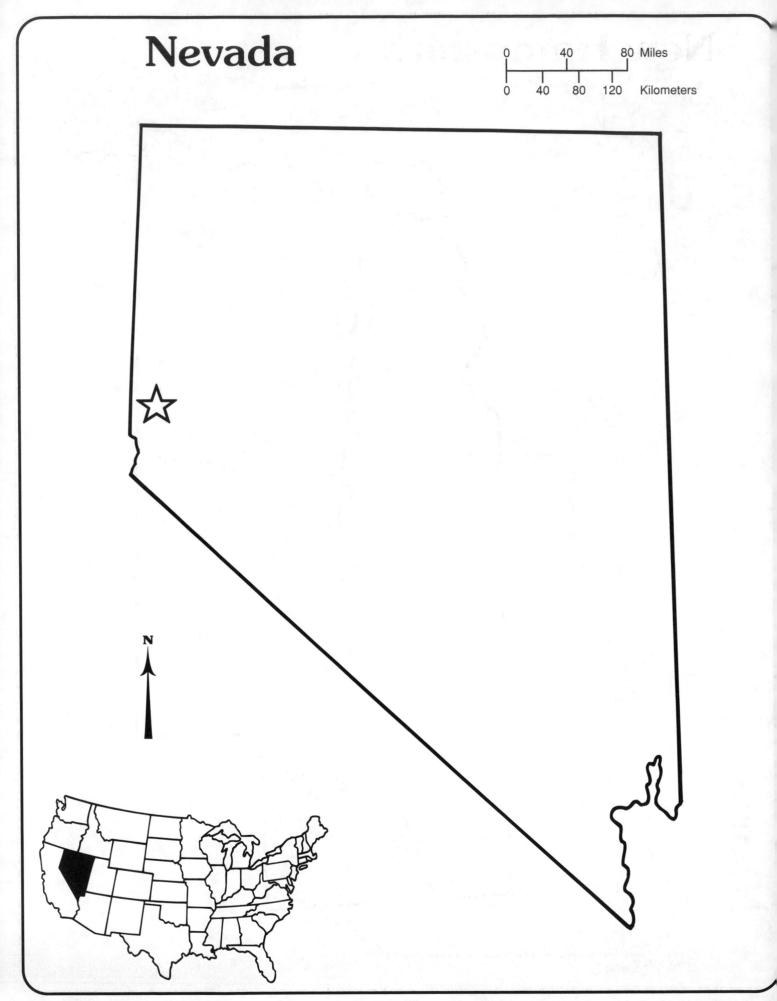

0   40   80 Miles

0   40   80   120   Kilometers

N

New Hampshire

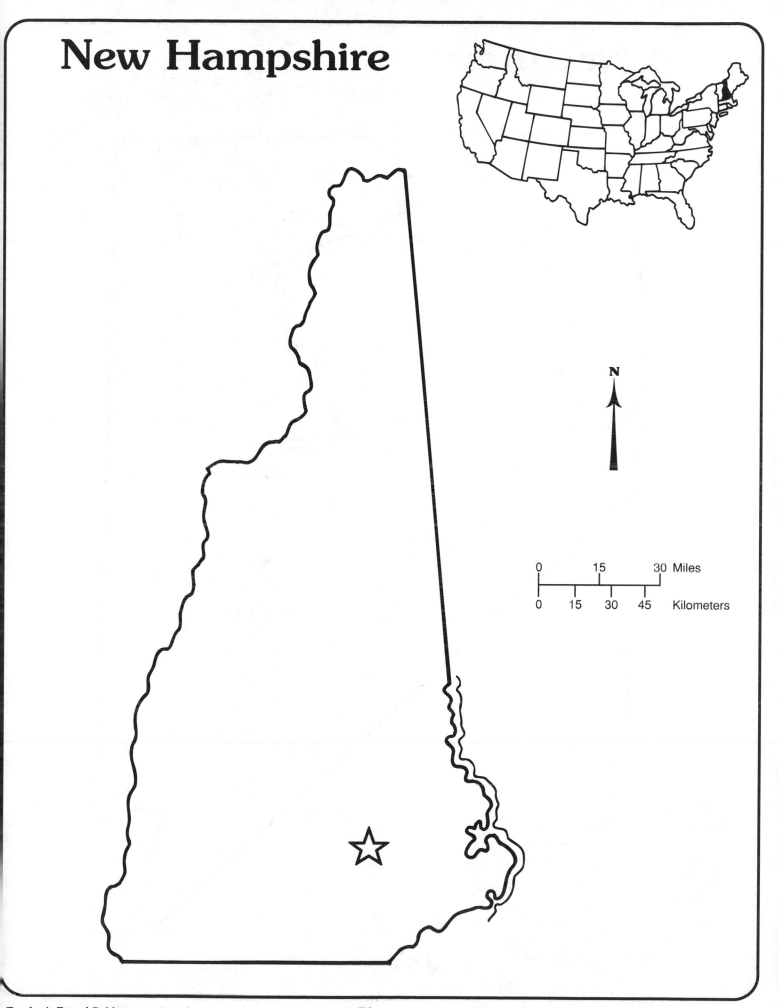

N

0		15		30 Miles

| 0 | 15 | 30 | 45 | Kilometers |

New Jersey

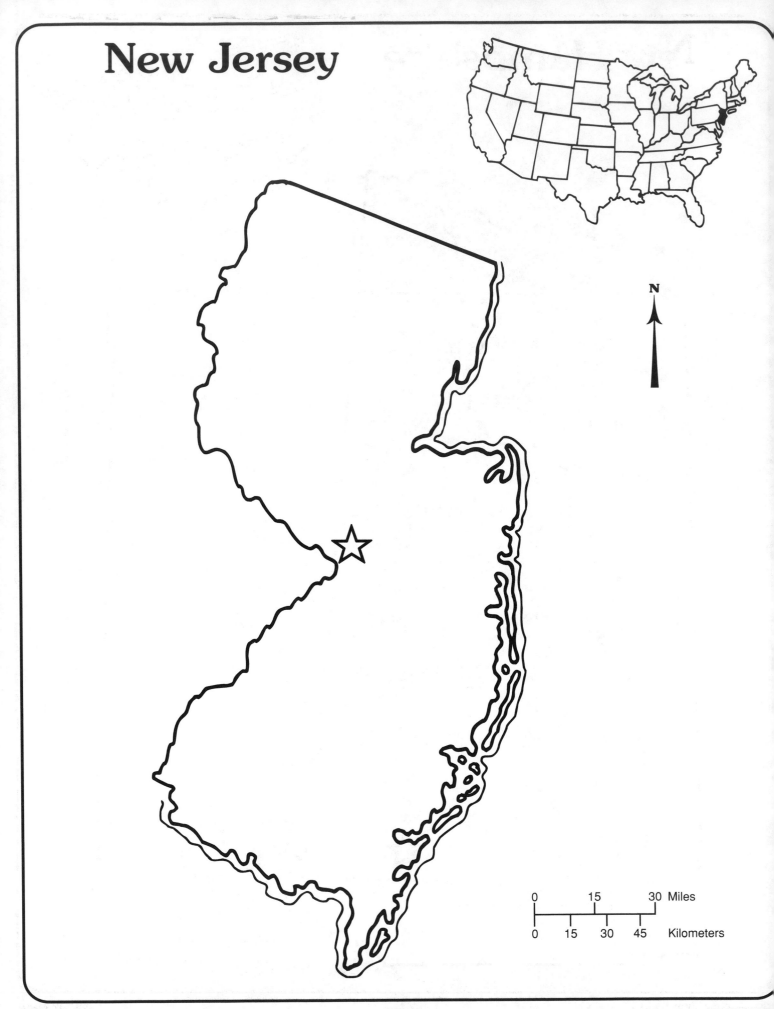

0   15   30 Miles

0   15   30   45   Kilometers

New Mexico

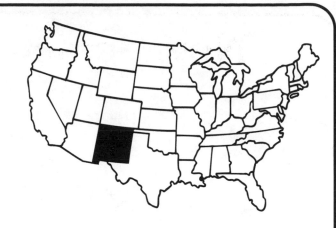

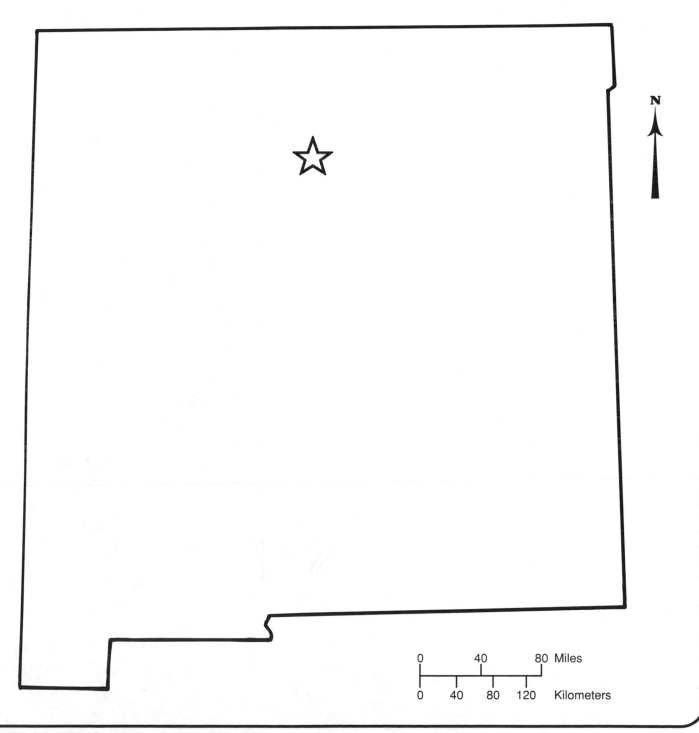

N

0	40	80 Miles
0	40	80	120	Kilometers

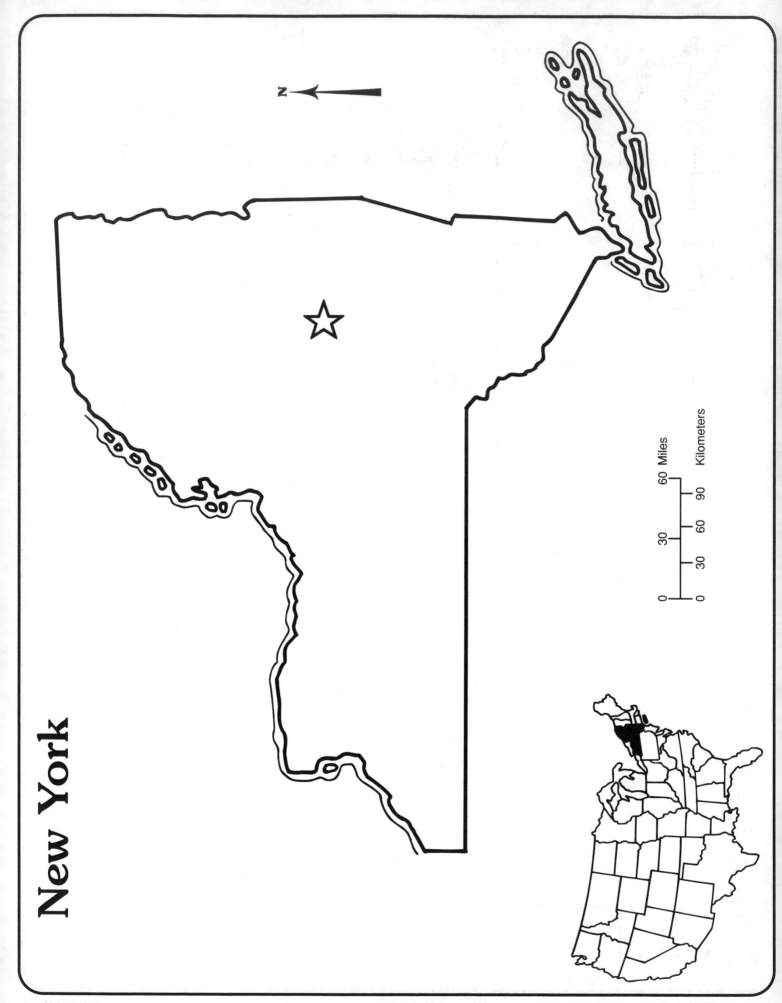

New York

N

60 Miles

Kilometers

30
0

90
60
30
0

North Carolina

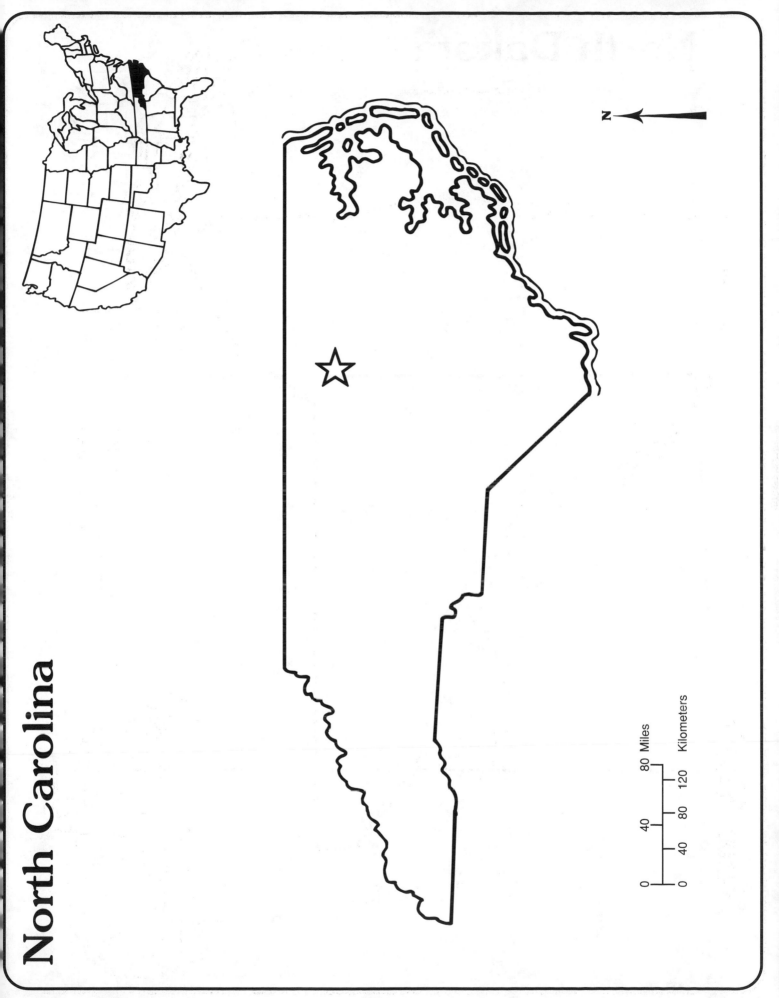

N

80 Miles

Kilometers

120

80

40

40

0

0

North Dakota

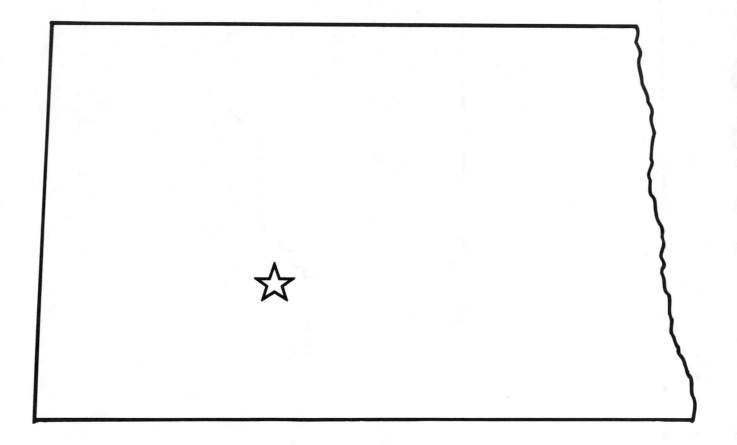

N

0		30		60 Miles
0	30	60	90	Kilometers

Ohio

0   25   50 Miles

0   25   50   75   Kilometers

N

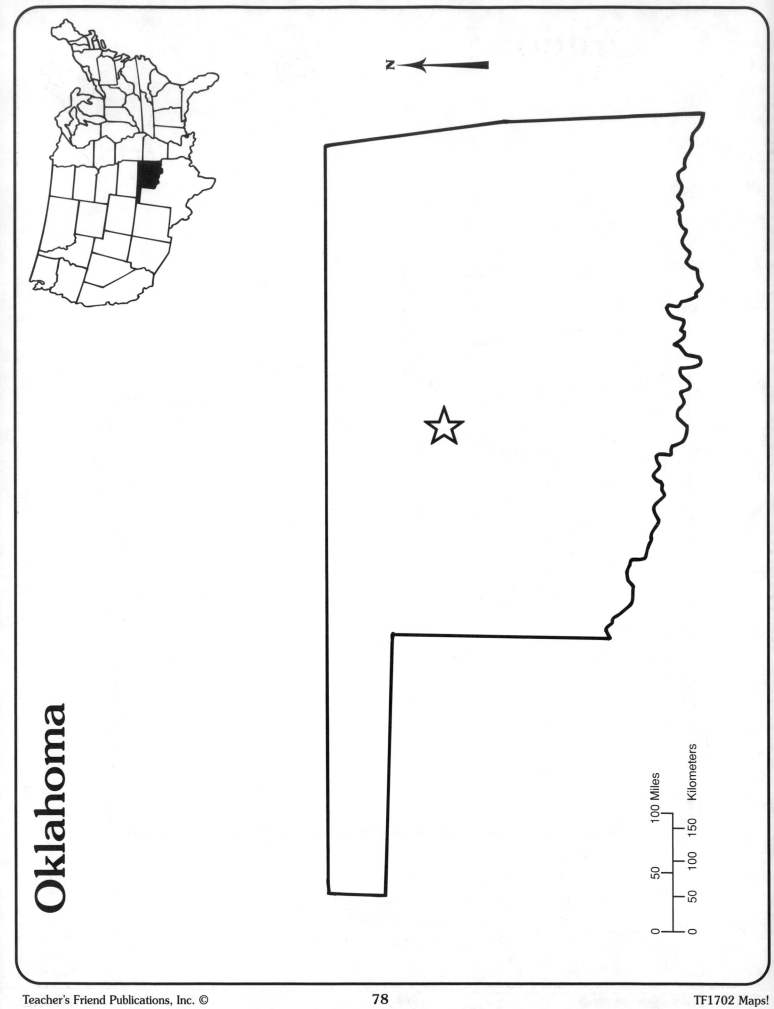

Oklahoma

N ←

☆

100 Miles

50

Kilometers
150
100
50
0

Oregon

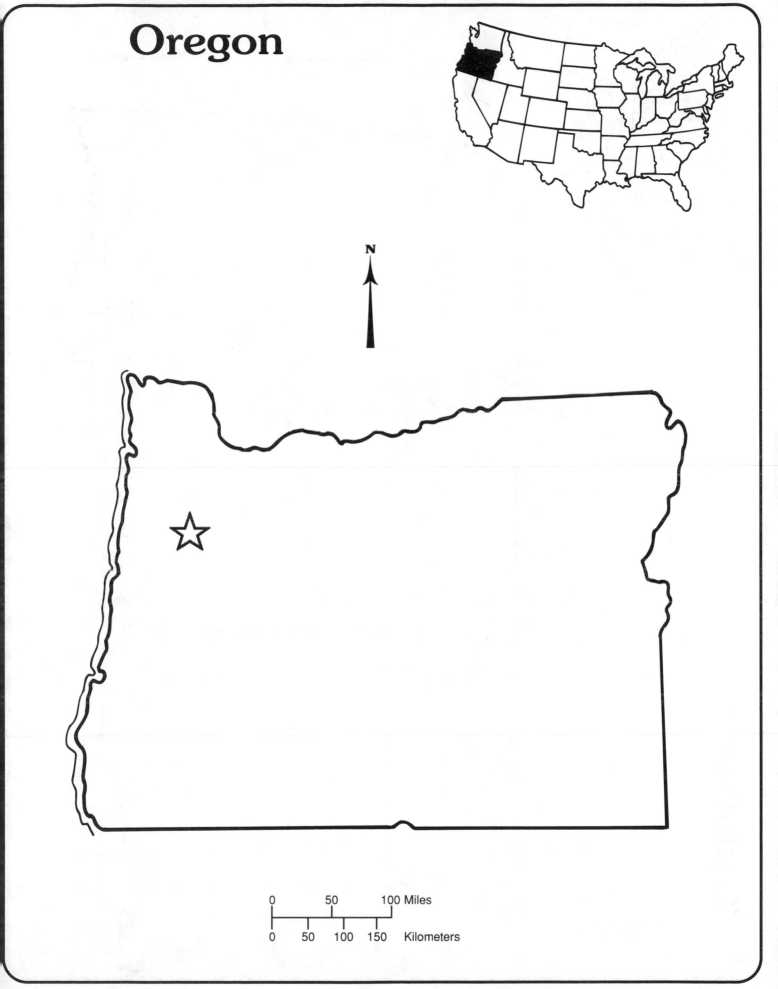

N

0   50   100 Miles

0   50   100 150   Kilometers

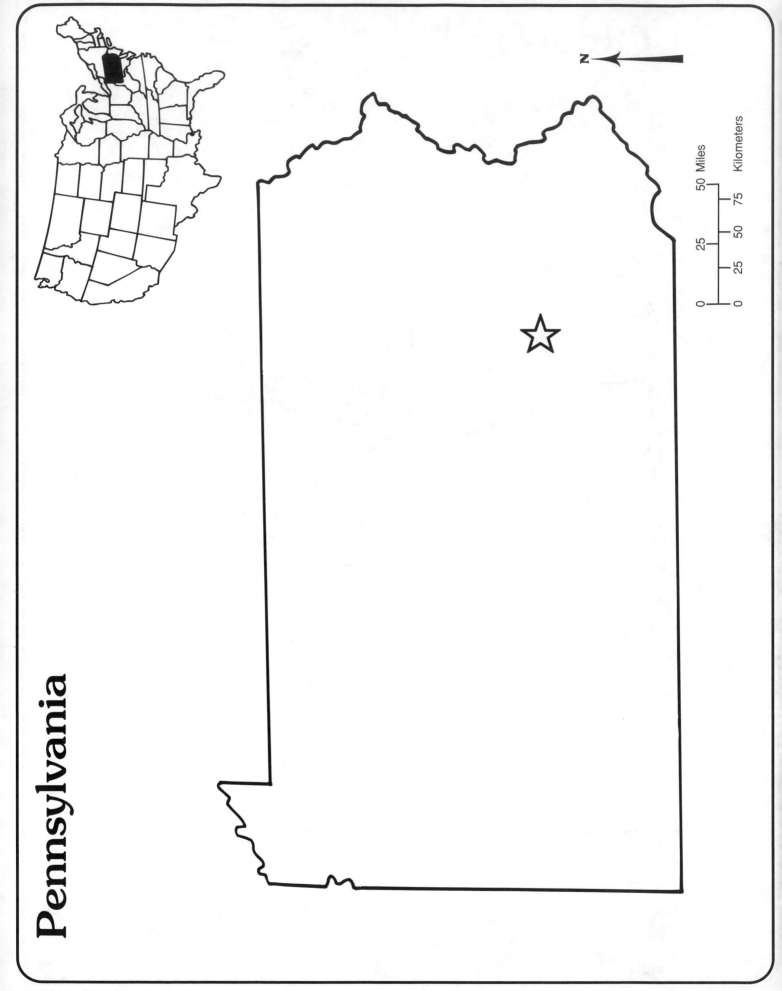

Pennsylvania

N

50 Miles
25
0

Kilometers
75
50
25
0

Rhode Island

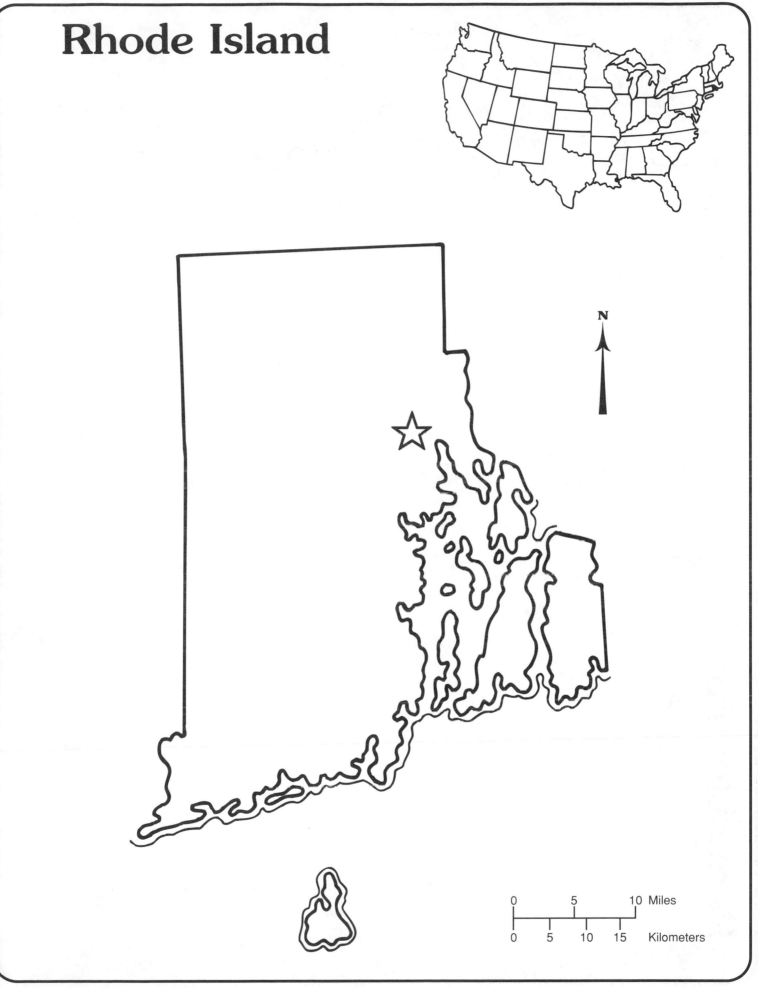

0   5   10 Miles

0   5   10   15   Kilometers

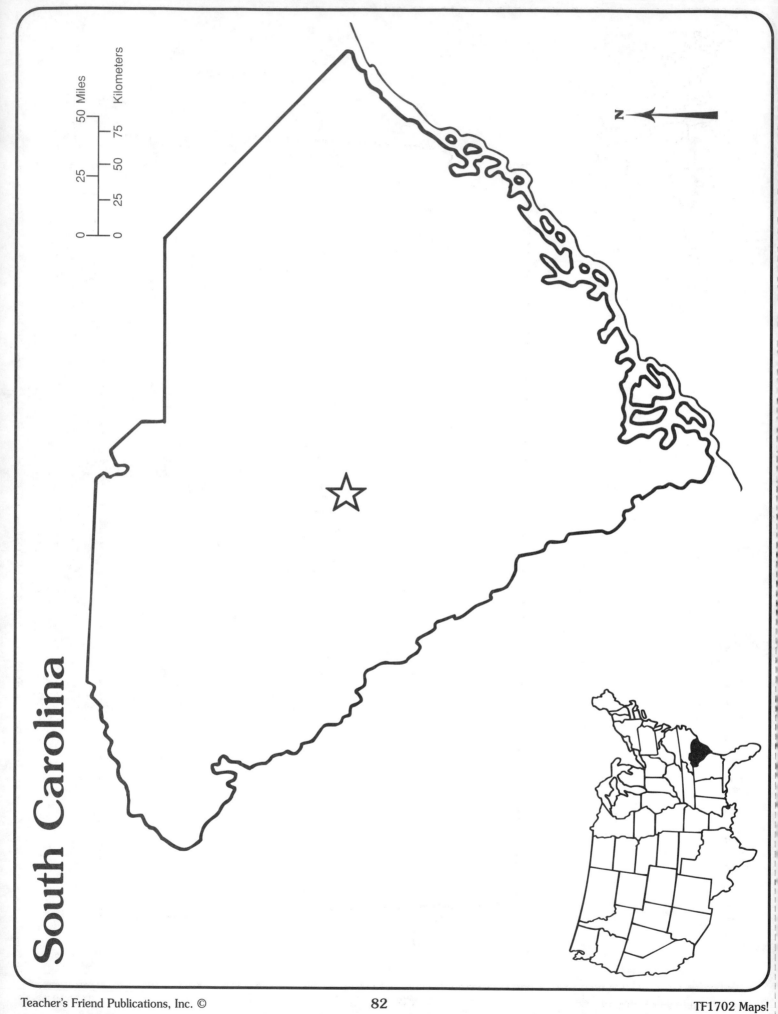

South Carolina

50 Miles
Kilometers
50
75
25
50
25
25
0
0

N

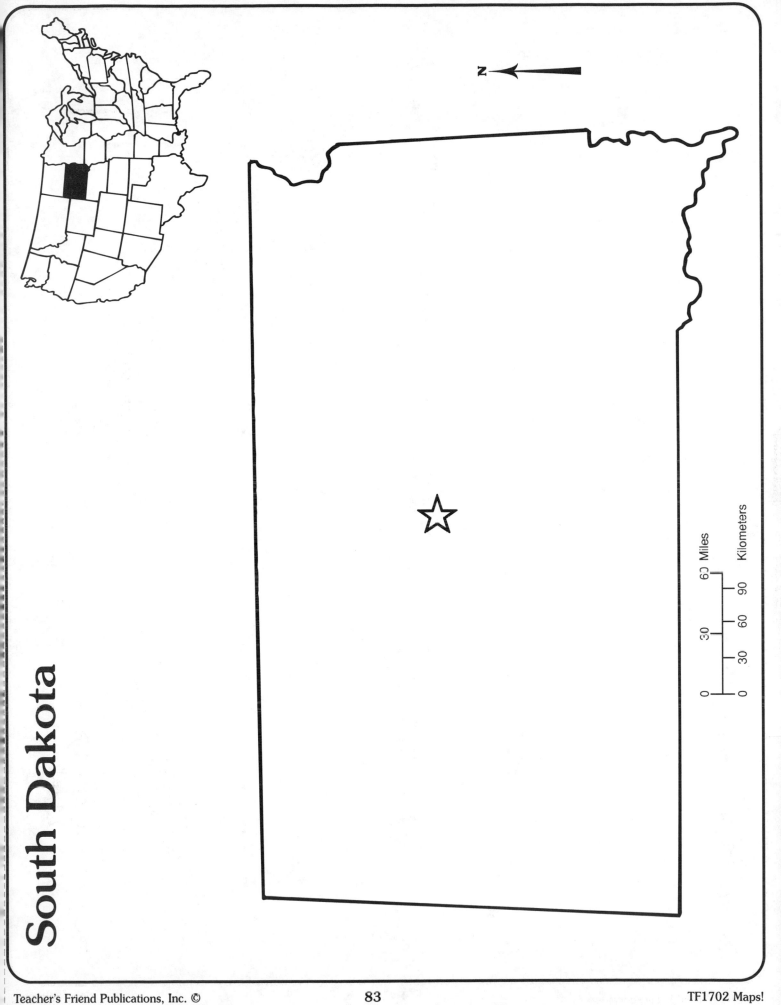

South Dakota

N

Miles
Kilometers

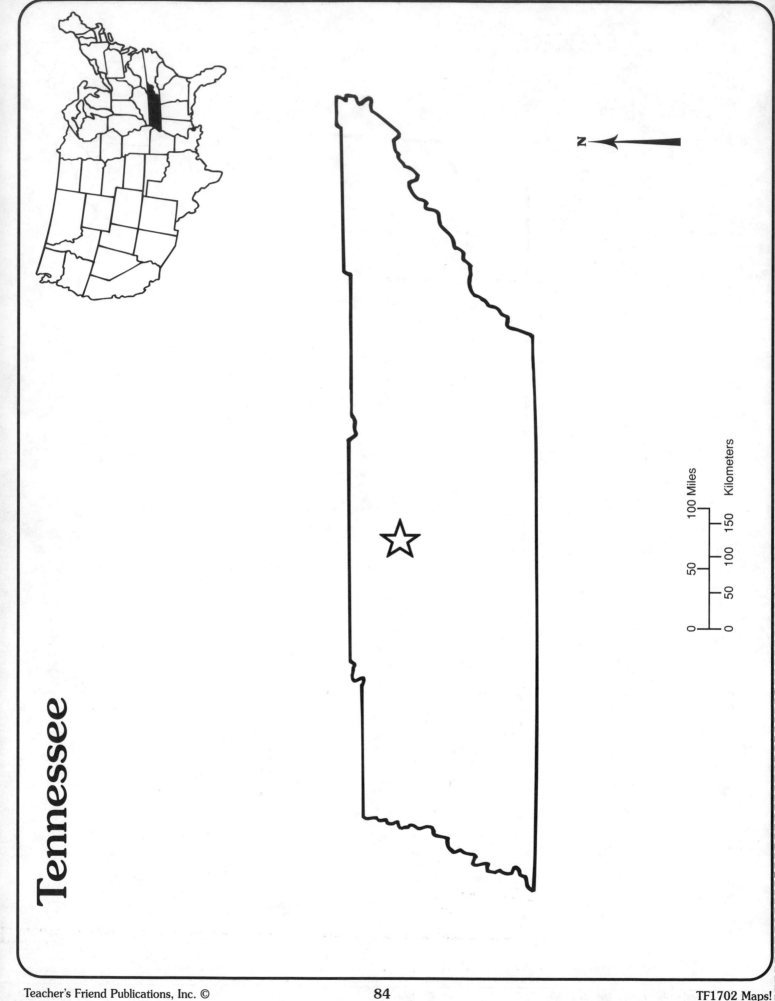

Tennessee

N

100 Miles

Kilometers

50

50

150

100

50

100

0

0

Texas

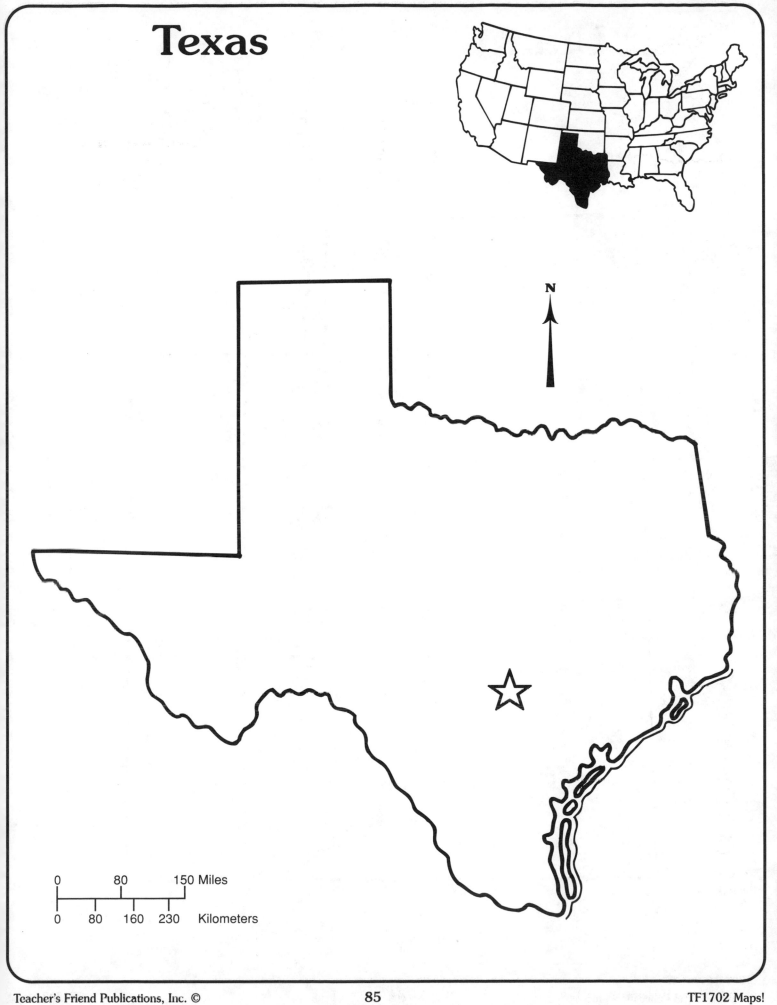

0   80   150 Miles

0   80   160   230   Kilometers

Utah

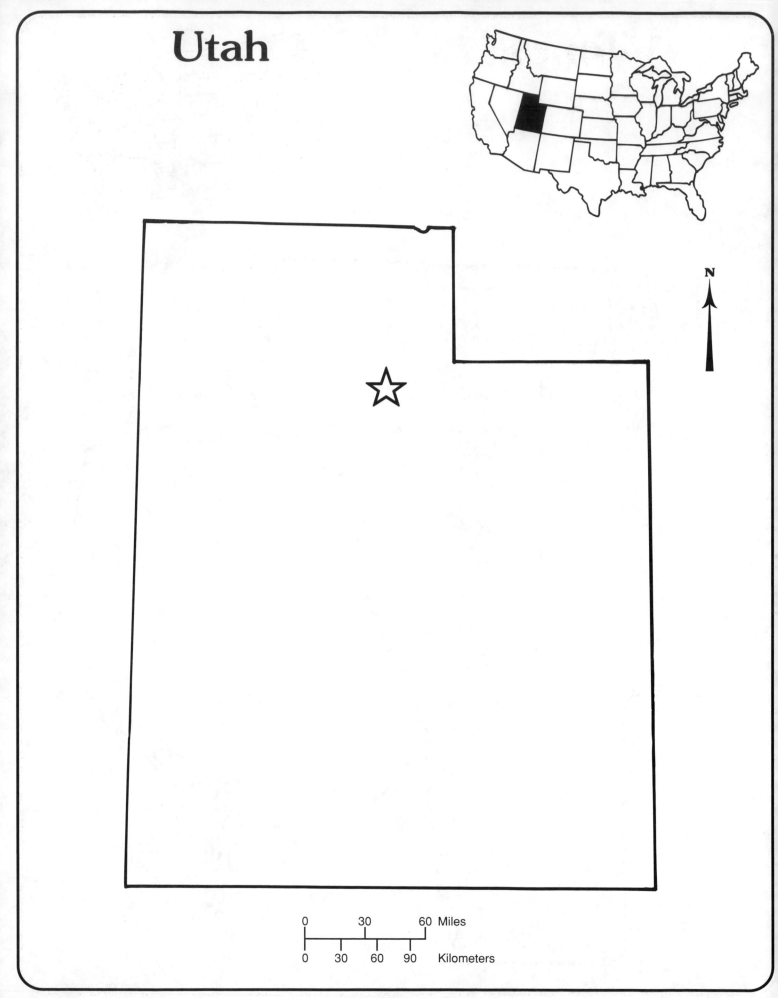

0   30   60 Miles

0   30   60   90   Kilometers

Vermont

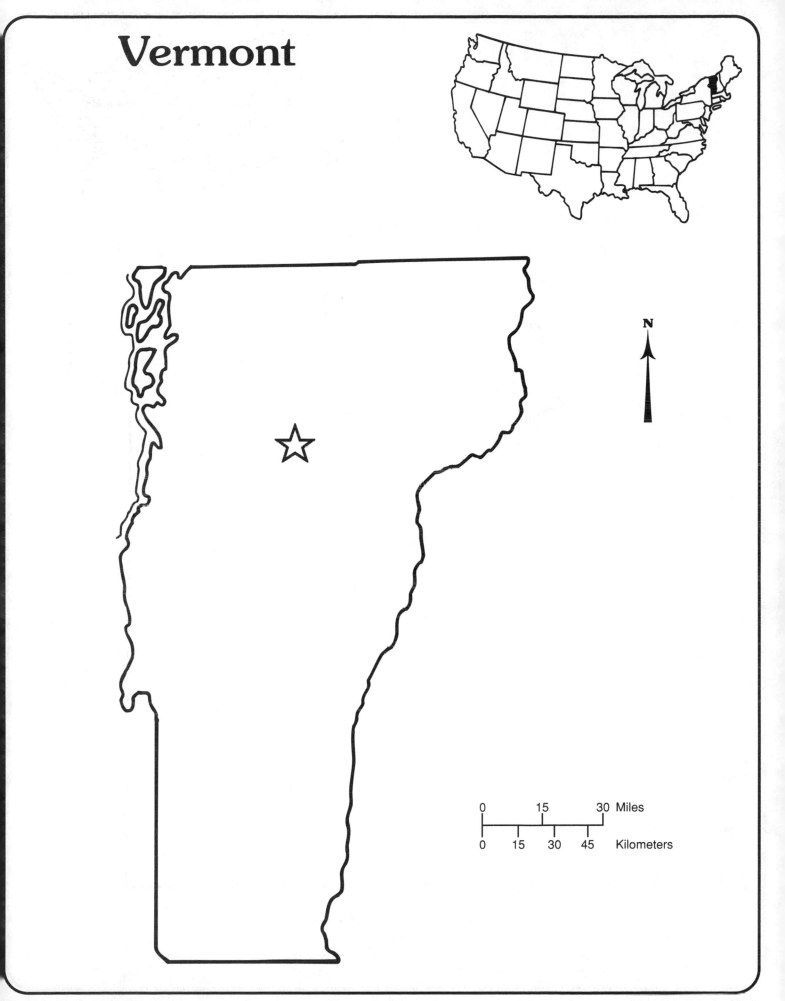

0   15   30 Miles

0   15   30   45   Kilometers

N

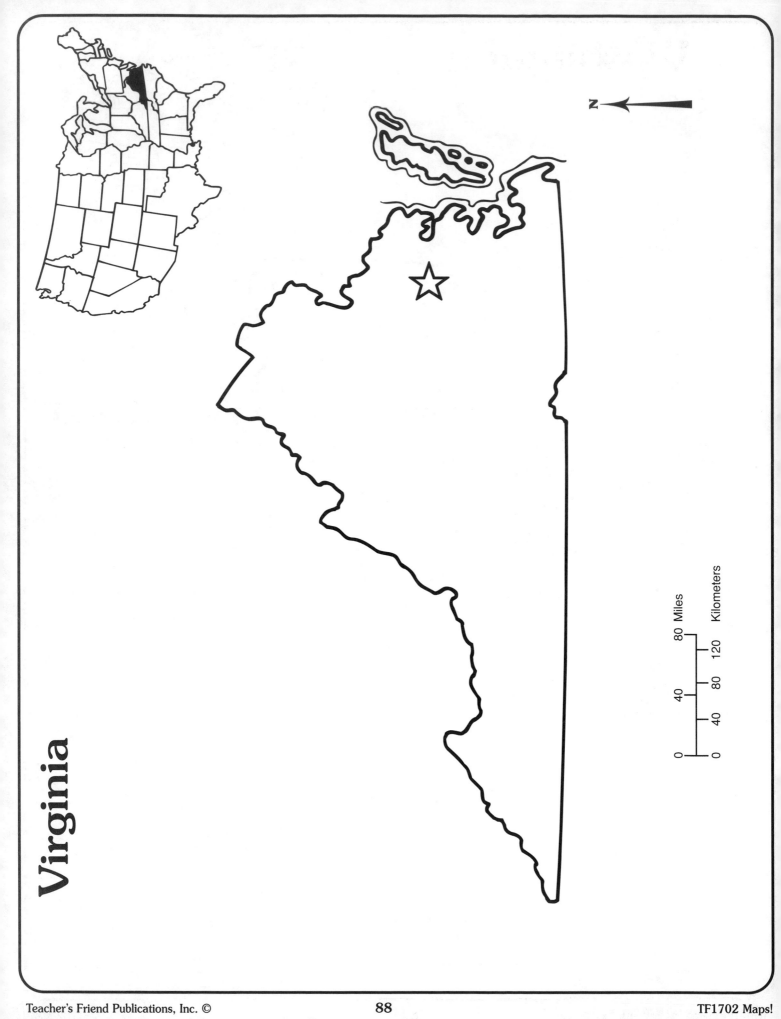

Virginia

N

80 Miles

Kilometers

120

40   80

40

0   0

Washington

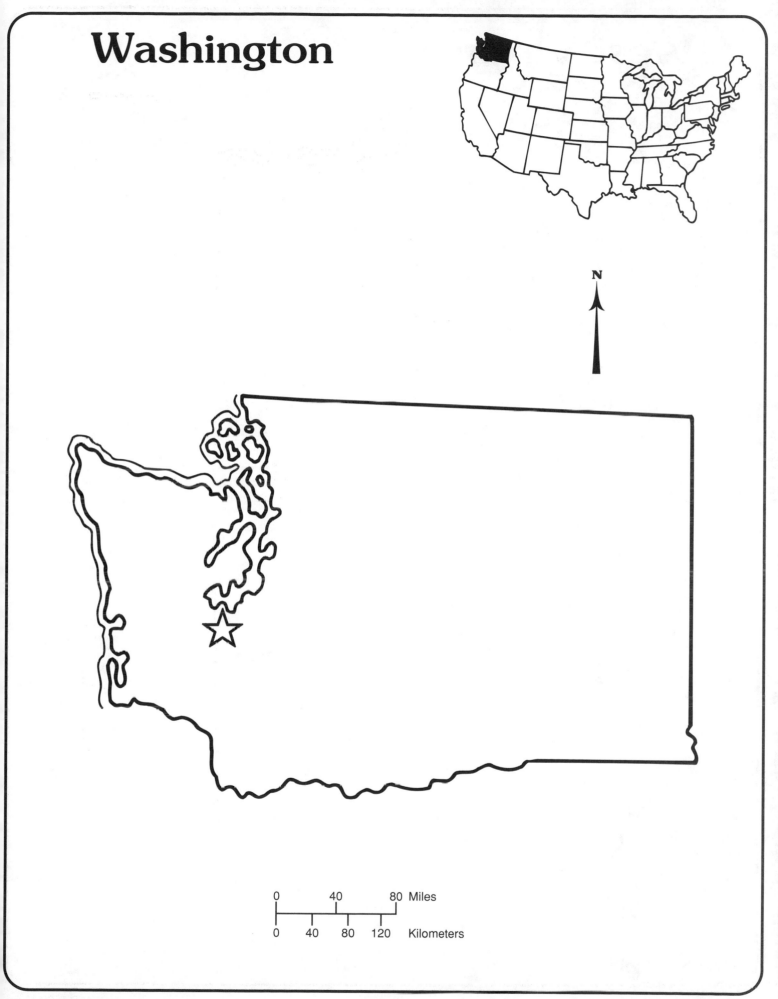

N

0   40   80 Miles

0   40   80   120   Kilometers

West Virginia

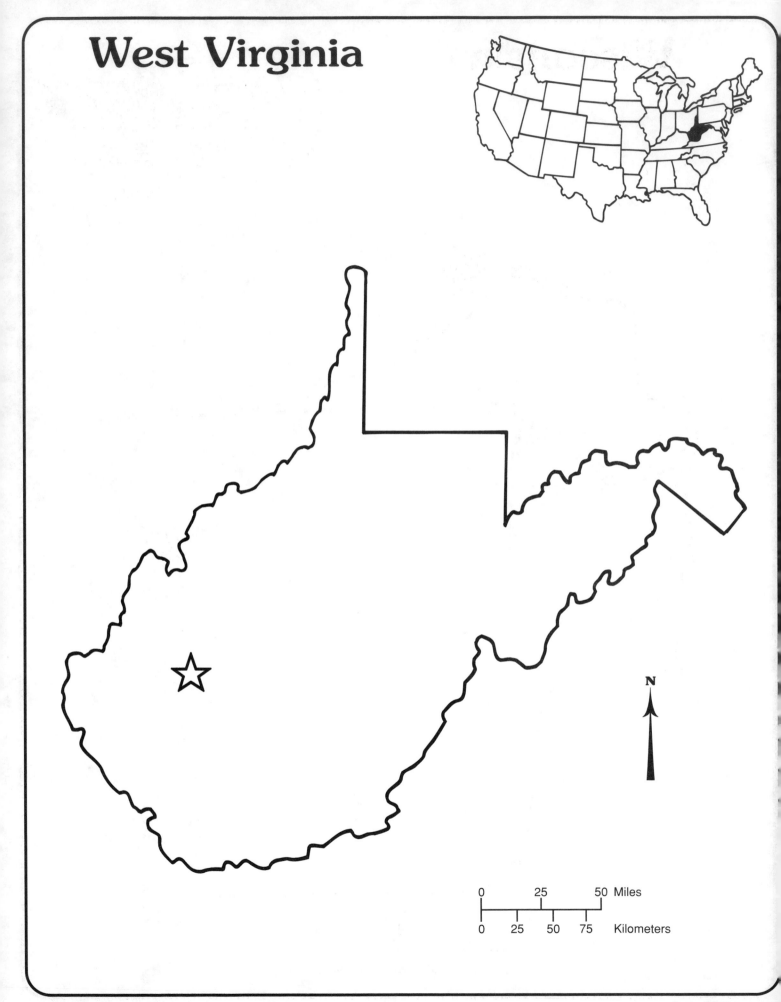

N

0		25		50 Miles

0	25	50	75	Kilometers

Wisconsin

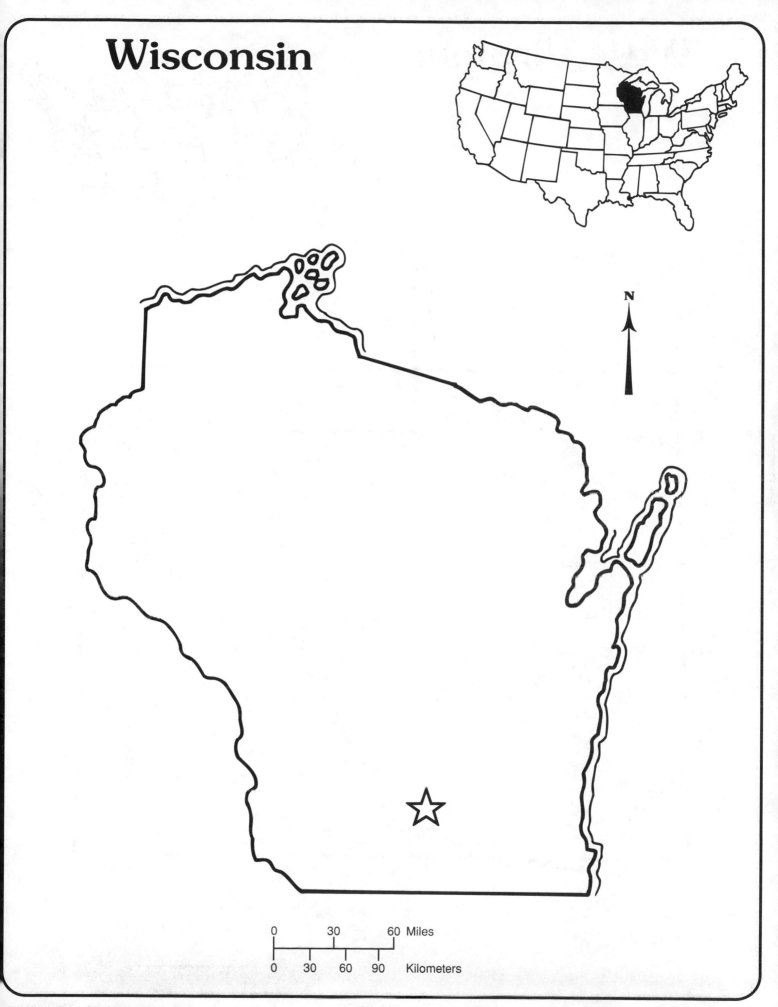

0   30   60 Miles

0   30   60   90   Kilometers

Wyoming

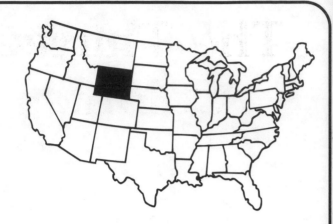

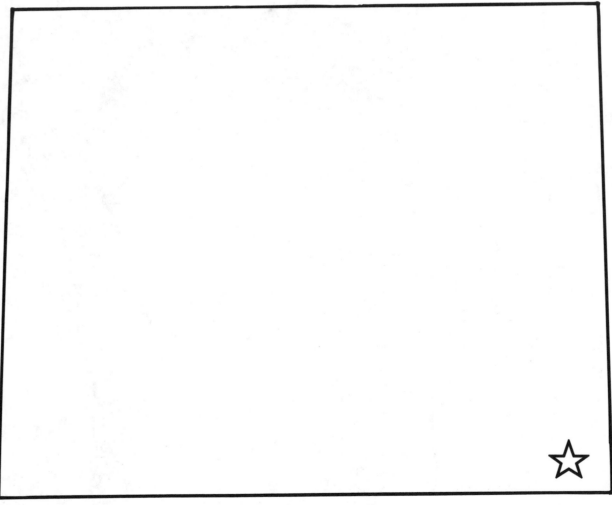

N

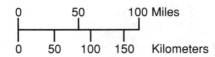

0   50   100 Miles

0   50   100   150   Kilometers

The Thirteen Colonies

N

New Hampshire

New York

Massachusetts

Rhode Island

Connecticut

Pennsylvania

New Jersey

Maryland

Delaware

Virginia

North Carolina

South Carolina

Georgia

The Thirteen Colonies

Regions of the U.S.

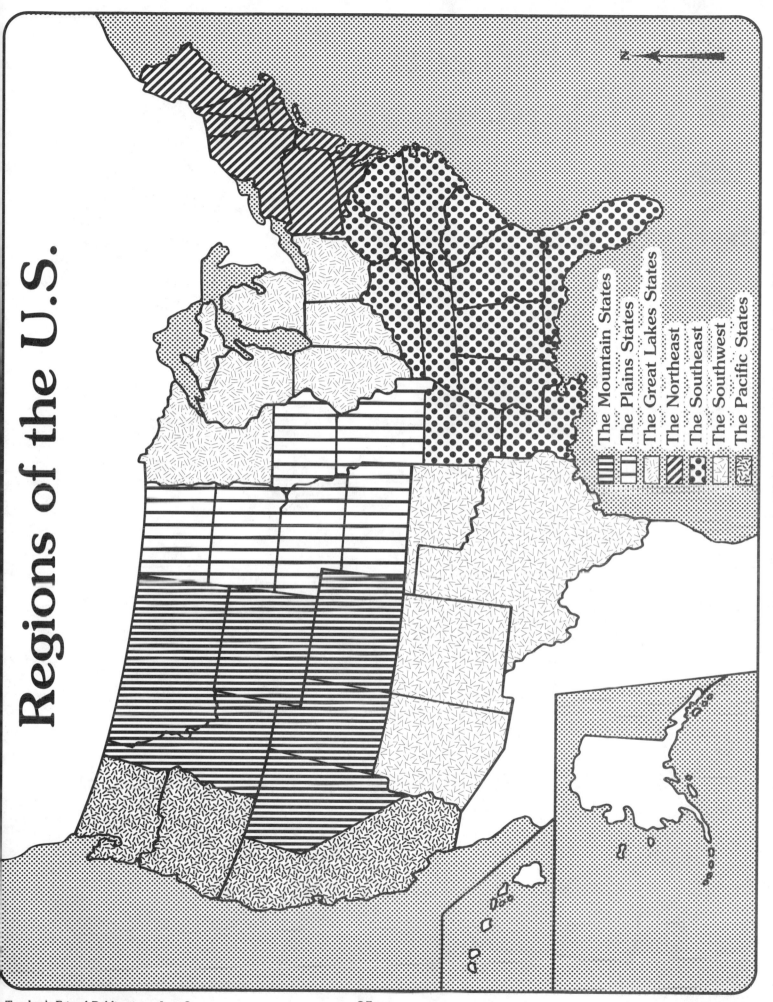

The Mountain States
The Plains States
The Great Lakes States
The Northeast
The Southeast
The Southwest
The Pacific States

U.S. Major Rivers and Lakes

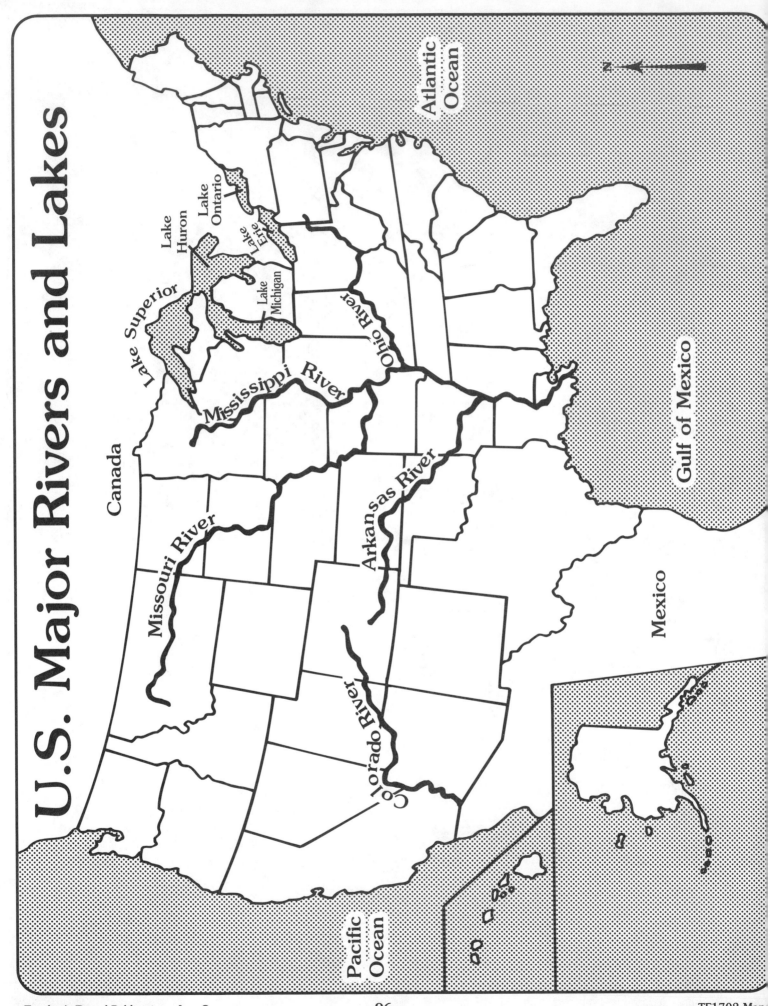

Atlantic Ocean

Lake Ontario

Lake Huron

Lake Erie

Lake Superior

Lake Michigan

Ohio River

Mississippi River

Canada

Missouri River

Arkansas River

Colorado River

Gulf of Mexico

Mexico

Pacific Ocean

N

Major U.S. Mountain Ranges and Deserts

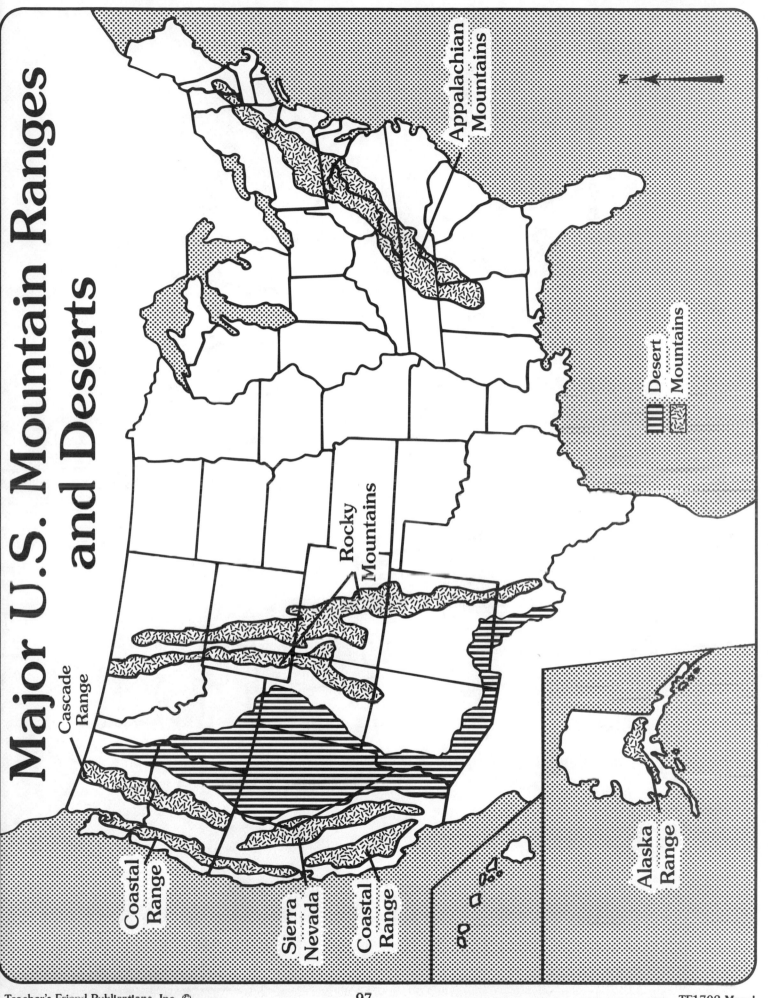

Appalachian Mountains

Rocky Mountains

Cascade Range

Coastal Range

Sierra Nevada

Coastal Range

Alaska Range

Desert

Mountains

N

U.S. Time Zones

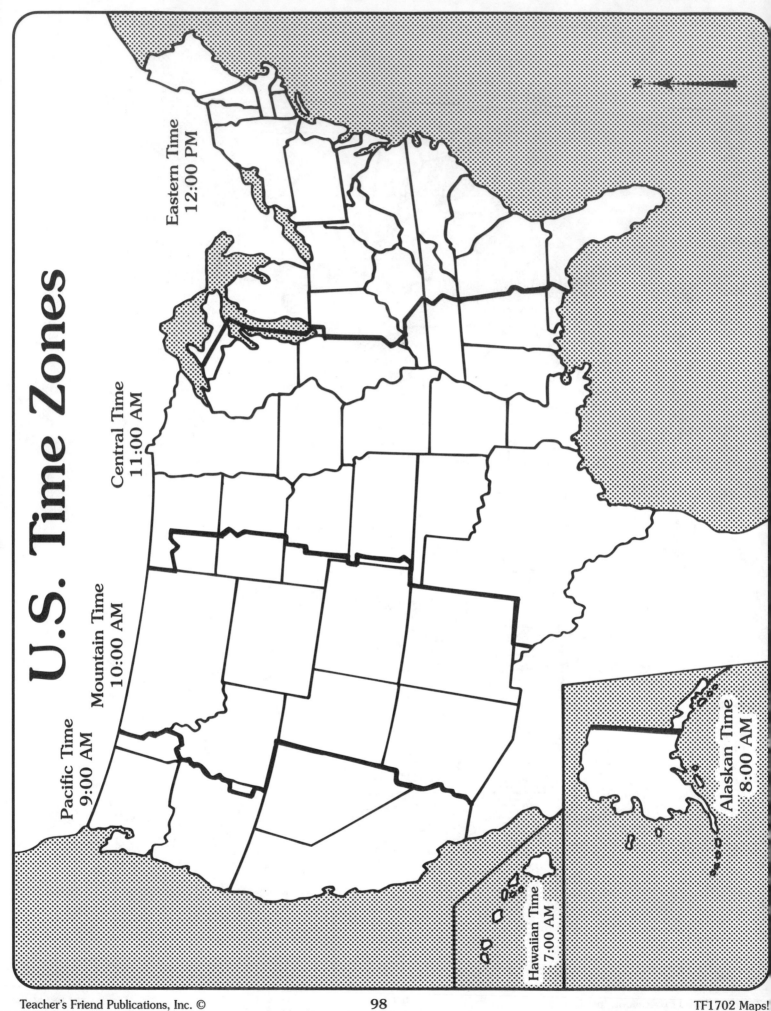

Pacific Time
9:00 AM

Mountain Time
10:00 AM

Central Time
11:00 AM

Eastern Time
12:00 PM

Alaskan Time
8:00 AM

Hawaiian Time
7:00 AM

NAME: _____ DATE: _____

MY STATE REPORT!

State Name: _____

State Capital: _____

Population: _____

Date of Statehood: _____

State Flag

State Seal

State Flower

State Bird

State Motto: _____

_____

State Nickname: _____

_____

Area: _____

Major Rivers and/or Lakes:

_____   _____

_____   _____

Major Mountains and/or Deserts:

_____   _____

_____   _____

National Parks:

_____   _____

_____   _____

Coastline: _____

Major Cities:

_____   _____

_____   _____

_____   _____

Major Industries:

_____   _____

_____   _____

Major Attractions:

_____   _____

_____   _____

Important Dates and Events:

_____   _____

_____   _____

_____   _____

_____   _____

_____   _____

_____   _____

_____   _____

_____   _____

State Information

ALABAMA
Capital: Montgomery
Admission Date: Dec. 14, 1819
State Flower: camellia
State Bird: yellowhammer
State Nickname: Heart of Dixie or
The Cotton State
State Motto: "We Dare Defend Our Rights"

ALASKA
Capital: Juneau
Admission Date: Jan. 3, 1959
State Flower: forget-me-not
State Bird: willow ptarmigan
State Nickname: The Last Frontier or Great Land
State Motto: "North to the Future"

ARIZONA
Capital: Phoenix
Admission Date: Feb. 14, 1912
State Flower: saguaro blossom
State Bird: cactus wren
State Nickname: Grand Canyon State
State Motto: "God Enriches"

ARKANSAS
Capital: Little Rock
Admission Date: June 15, 1836
State Flower: apple blossom
State Bird: mockingbird
State Nickname: Land of Opportunity or
Razorback State
State Motto: "The People Rule"

CALIFORNIA
Capital: Sacramento
Admission Date: Sept. 9, 1850
State Flower: golden poppy
State Bird: California valley quail
State Nickname: Golden State
State Motto: "'Eureka!' (I Have Found It!)"

COLORADO
Capital: Denver
Admission Date: Aug. 1, 1876
State Flower: blue columbine
State Bird: lark bunting
State Nickname: Centennial State
State Motto: "Nothing Without Providence"

CONNECTICUT
Capital: Hartford
Admission Date: Jan. 9, 1788
State Flower: mountain laurel
State Bird: American robin
State Nickname: The Nutmeg State or
The Constitution State
State Motto: "He Who Transplanted Still Sustains"

DELAWARE
Capital: Dover
Admission Date: Dec. 7, 1787
State Flower: peach blossom
State Bird: blue hen chicken
State Nickname: The First State or
The Diamond State
State Motto: "Liberty and Independence"

FLORIDA
Capital: Tallahassee
Admission Date: March 3, 1845
State Flower: orange blossom
State Bird: mockingbird
State Nickname: The Sunshine State
State Motto: "In God We Trust"

GEORGIA
Capital: Atlanta
Admission Date: Jan. 2, 1788
State Flower: Cherokee rose
State Bird: brown thrasher
State Nickname: The Empire State of the South or
The Peach State
State Motto: "Wisdom, Justice, and Moderation"

HAWAII
Capital: Honolulu
Admission Date: Aug. 21, 1959
State Flower: hibiscus
State Bird: Hawaiian goose
State Nickname: Aloha State
State Motto: "The Life of the Land is Perpetuated
in Righteousness"

IDAHO
Capital: Boise
Admission Date: July 3, 1890
State Flower: syringa (mock orange)
State Bird: mountain bluebird
State Nickname: Gem State
State Motto: "It is Perpetual"

ILLINOIS
Capital: Springfield
Admission Date: Dec. 3, 1818
State Flower: violet
State Bird: cardinal
State Nickname: Land of Lincoln or Prairie State
State Motto: "State Sovereignty, National Union"

INDIANA
Capital: Indianapolis
Admission Date: Dec. 11, 1816
State Flower: peony
State Bird: cardinal
State Nickname: Hoosier State
State Motto: "The Crossroads of America"

IOWA
Capital: Des Moines
Admission Date: Dec. 28, 1846
State Flower: wild rose
State Bird: goldfinch
State Nickname: The Hawkeye State
State Motto: "Our Liberties We Prize and
Our Rights We Will Maintain"

KANSAS
Capital: Topeka
Admission Date: Jan. 29, 1861
State Flower: sunflower
State Bird: western meadowlark
State Nickname: Sunflower State or Jayhawk State
State Motto: "To the Stars Through Difficulties"

KENTUCKY
Capital: Frankfort
Admission Date: June 1, 1792
State Flower: goldenrod
State Bird: cardinal
State Nickname: The Bluegrass State
State Motto: "United We Stand, Divided We Fall"

LOUISIANA
Capital: Baton Rouge
Admission Date: April 30, 1812
State Flower: magnolia
State Bird: eastern brown pelican
State Nickname: The Pelican State or
The Creole State
State Motto: "Union, Justice and Confidence"

MAINE
Capital: Augusta
Admission Date: March 15, 1820
State Flower: white pine cone
State Bird: chickadee
State Nickname: The Pine Tree State
State Motto: "I Direct"

MARYLAND
Capital: Annapolis
Admission Date: April 28, 1788
State Flower: black-eyed susan
State Bird: Baltimore oriole
State Nickname: The Old Line State
State Motto: "Manly Deeds, Womanly Words"

MASSACHUSETTS
Capital: Boston
Admission Date: Feb. 6, 1788
State Flower: mayflower (arbutus)
State Bird: chickadee
State Nickname: The Bay State or
The Old Colony State
State Motto: "By the Sword We Seek Peace,
but Peace Only Under Liberty"

MICHIGAN
Capital: Lansing
Admission Date: Jan. 26, 1837
State Flower: apple blossom
State Bird: robin
State Nickname: The Great Lake State or
The Wolverine State
State Motto: "If You Seek a Pleasant Peninsula,
Look About You"

MINNESOTA
Capital: Saint Paul
Admission Date: May 11, 1858
State Flower: pink and white lady's slipper
State Bird: common loon
State Nickname: Gopher State or North Star State
State Motto: "The Star of the North"

MISSISSIPPI
Capital: Jackson
Admission Date: Dec. 10, 1817
State Flower: magnolia
State Bird: mockingbird
State Nickname: The Magnolia State
State Motto: "By Valor and Arms"

MISSOURI
Capital: Jefferson City
Admission Date: Aug. 10, 1821
State Flower: hawthorn
State Bird: eastern bluebird
State Nickname: The Show Me State
State Motto: "The Welfare of the People Shall
Be the Supreme Law"

MONTANA
Capital: Helena
Admission Date: Nov. 8, 1889
State Flower: bitterroot
State Bird: western meadowlark
State Nickname: Treasure State
State Motto: "Gold and Silver"

NEBRASKA
Capital: Lincoln
Admission Date: March 1, 1867
State Flower: goldenrod
State Bird: western meadowlark
State Nickname: Cornhusker State
State Motto: "Equality Before the Law"

NEVADA
Capital: Carson City
Admission Date: Oct. 31, 1864
State Flower: sagebrush
State Bird: mountain bluebird
State Nickname: Sagebrush State or Silver State
State Motto: "All for Our Country"

NEW HAMPSHIRE
Capital: Concord
Admission Date: June 21, 1788
State Flower: purple lilac
State Bird: purple finch
State Nickname: The Granite State
State Motto: "Live Free or Die"

NEW JERSEY
Capital: Trenton
Admission Date: Dec. 18, 1787
State Flower: purple violet
State Bird: eastern goldfinch
State Nickname: The Garden State
State Motto: "Liberty and Prosperity"

NEW MEXICO
Capital: Santa Fe
Admission Date: Jan. 6, 1912
State Flower: yucca
State Bird: roadrunner
State Nickname: Land of Enchantment
State Motto: "It Grows as It Goes"

NEW YORK
Capital: Albany
Admission Date: July 26, 1788
State Flower: rose
State Bird: bluebird
State Nickname: The Empire State
State Motto: "'Excelsior' (Ever Upward)"

NORTH CAROLINA
Capital: Raleigh
Admission Date: Nov. 21, 1789
State Flower: dogwood
State Bird: cardinal
State Nickname: The Tar Heel State or
Old North State
State Motto: "To Be, Rather Than to Seem"

NORTH DAKOTA
Capital: Bismarck
Admission Date: Nov. 2, 1889
State Flower: wild prairie rose
State Bird: western meadowlark
State Nickname: Peace Garden State or Sioux State
State Motto: "Liberty and Union, Now and Forever, One and Inseparable"

OHIO
Capital: Columbus
Admission Date: March 1, 1803
State Flower: carnation
State Bird: cardinal
State Nickname: The Buckeye State
State Motto: "With God, All Things Are Possible"

OKLAHOMA
Capital: Oklahoma City
Admission Date: Nov. 16, 1907
State Flower: mistletoe
State Bird: scissor-tailed flycatcher
State Nickname: Sooner State
State Motto: "Labor Conquers All Things"

OREGON
Capital: Salem
Admission Date: Feb. 14, 1859
State Flower: Oregon grape
State Bird: western meadowlark
State Nickname: Beaver State
State Motto: "The Union"

PENNSYLVANIA
Capital: Harrisburg
Admission Date: Dec. 12, 1787
State Flower: mountain laurel
State Bird: ruffed grouse
State Nickname: The Keystone State
State Motto: "Virtue, Liberty and Independence"

RHODE ISLAND
Capital: Providence
Admission Date: May 29, 1790
State Flower: violet
State Bird: Rhode Island red
State Nickname: Little Rhody or The Ocean State
State Motto: "Hope"

SOUTH CAROLINA
Capital: Columbia
Admission Date: May 23, 1788
State Flower: Carolina jessamine
State Bird: Carolina wren
State Nickname: Palmetto State
State Motto: "While I Breathe, I Hope"

SOUTH DAKOTA
Capital: Pierre
Admission Date: Nov. 2, 1889
State Flower: pasque flower
State Bird: ring-necked pheasant
State Nickname: Sunshine State or Coyote State
State Motto: "Under God the People Rule"

TENNESSEE
Capital: Nashville
Admission Date: June 1, 1796
State Flower: iris
State Bird: mockingbird
State Nickname: The Volunteer State
State Motto: "Agriculture and Commerce" or "Tennessee--America at Its Best"

TEXAS
Capital: Austin
Admission Date: Dec. 29, 1845
State Flower: bluebonnet
State Bird: mockingbird
State Nickname: Lone Star State
State Motto: "Friendship"

UTAH
Capital: Salt Lake City
Admission Date: Jan. 4, 1896
State Flower: sego lily
State Bird: seagull
State Nickname: Beehive State
State Motto: "Industry"

VERMONT
Capital: Montpelier
Admission Date: March 4, 1791
State Flower: red clover
State Bird: hermit thrush
State Nickname: The Green Mountain State
State Motto: "Freedom and Unity"

VIRGINIA
Capital: Richmond
Admission Date: June 25, 1788
State Flower: dogwood
State Bird: cardinal
State Nickname: The Old Dominion--Mother of Presidents
State Motto: "Thus Always to Tyrants"

WASHINGTON
Capital: Olympia
Admission Date: Nov. 11, 1889
State Flower: rhododendron
State Bird: willow goldfinch
State Nickname: Evergreen State
State Motto: "By and By"

WEST VIRGINIA
Capital: Charleston
Admission Date: June 20, 1863
State Flower: rhododendron
State Bird: cardinal
State Nickname: The Mountain State
State Motto: "Mountaineers Are Always Free"

WISCONSIN
Capital: Madison
Admission Date: May 29, 1848
State Flower: wood violet
State Bird: robin
State Nickname: The Badger State
State Motto: "Forward"

WYOMING
Capital: Cheyenne
Admission Date: July 10, 1890
State Flower: Indian paintbrush
State Bird: meadowlark
State Nickname: Equality State
State Motto: "Equal Rights"